I0605063

PRAISE FOR *TITAN UNFINISHED*

"Part memoir, part business narrative, and part media autopsy, *Titan Unfinished* plunges readers deep into a visionary venture turned global headline—from a co-founder who lived it. For entrepreneurs and PR professionals, it's a rare, unflinching look at what happens when innovation meets tragedy and the narrative gets hijacked—offering urgent lessons in leadership, message control, and the cost of silence."

—David Meerman Scott, Bestselling Author, *The New Rules of Marketing and PR*

"Pushing the edge of technology is never easy—especially when lives are on the line. Whether it's spaceships or submarines, venturing beyond today's edge into tomorrow's routine is always a dangerous place to be. And yet, there are always those bold enough to take the ride.

This is a human tale, and humans can be both right and wrong. The same boldness that drives innovation can also be an Achilles' heel. In a world where headlines are written for clicks more than truth, Guillermo takes us inside the *Titan* story—as both a founder and a friend of the sub's designer. We mourn. We learn. And still, we reach beyond the known."

—Rick Tumlinson, Founder, SpaceFund and EarthLight Foundation

"After hearing so much about the importance of safety from my father throughout all his submarine exploration, I was in shock to learn about the *Titan* disaster. Thanks to this book, we will finally understand what happened!"

—Dr. Bertrand Piccard, Explorer and President, Solar Impulse Foundation

"A gripping and intensely personal look inside the submersible company Oceangate, centering on its mastermind leader, Stockton Rush. No one but Söhnlein could tell the story here, and he does so deftly, in a deeply engaging read. I highly recommend it."

—Dr. Alan Stern, Planetary Scientist, Commercial Astronaut, and Titanic Explorer

TITAN UNFINISHED

TITAN UNFINISHED

An Untold Story of Exploration, Innovation, and the OceanGate Tragedy

Guillermo A. M. Söhnlein

Matt Holt Books
An Imprint of BenBella Books, Inc.
Dallas, TX

Matt Holt is an imprint of BenBella Books, Inc.
8080 N. Central Expressway
Suite 1700
Dallas, TX 75206
benbellabooks.com
Send feedback to feedback@benbellabooks.com

Printed in the United States of America
10 9 8 7 6 5 4 3 2 1

Library of Congress Control Number: 2025020880
ISBN 9781637747674 (hardcover)
ISBN 9781637747681 (electronic)

Editing by Lydia Choi
Copyediting by Amy Handy
Proofreading by Denise Pangia and Cheryl Beacham
Text design and composition by Aaron Edmiston
Cover design by Brigid Pearson
Cover photo by Becky Kagan Schott
Printed by Lake Book Manufacturing

For the 2023 Titanic Expedition Mission 5 crew,
who gave their lives in pursuit of exploration,
and their loved ones and the extended OceanGate family
that suffered the pain of their loss.

CONTENTS

LIST OF ACRONYMS

ABS	American Bureau of Shipping
ATM	Atmosphere (unit of measurement for atmospheric pressure)
AUV	Autonomous Underwater Vehicle
CBP	Customs and Border Protection
DEA	Drug Enforcement Administration
DNV	Det Norske Veritas (Norwegian company)
DOD	Department of Defense
DON	Department of the Navy
ISS	International Space Station
LRT	Launch, Retrieval, and Transportation System
MTS	Marine Technology Society
MUV	Manned Underwater Vehicles
NASA	National Aeronautics and Space Administration
NAVIC	Navigation and Vessel Inspection Circular
NOAA	National Oceanic and Atmospheric Administration
NTSB	National Transportation Safety Board
ORV	Oceanographic Research Vessel
ROV	Remotely Operated Vehicle
TEC	The Explorers Club
UI	Underwater Intervention
USCG	United States Coast Guard

FOREWORD

June 28, 2025
Falmouth, Massachusetts

In June 2023, while the world was transfixed by the desperate search for the submersible *Titan*, I was far from the action—and deeply frustrated. Normally, I would have been on the air, helping audiences understand the nuances of science, technology, and the lure of pushing both to the ragged edge of possibility. But I was thirteen time zones away—on assignment in Japan, at the site of another cautionary tale: the Fukushima Daiichi nuclear power plant.

The Japanese government was poised to release water tainted with radioactive tritium into the Pacific Ocean. The announcement triggered a blizzard of wild, inaccurate allegations on social media and in some corners of the legacy press. I was there with *PBS NewsHour*, trying to sort fact from fiction—to interview scientific experts, tour the site, and produce an accurate account of the decision's rationale and its real environmental impact.

As I worked to cut through one swirl of misinformation, I watched another one spiral out of control in real time: the *Titan* story.

After long, hot days of filming wearing hazmat suits, respirators, and gloves to protect against radiation and contamination, I returned to my hotel and a steady, disheartening stream of fake news.

Social media and mainstream outlets alike elevated a fabricated transcript of the *Titan* crew's "final moments"—a gripping but wholly invented account of panic, system failures, and desperate radio calls that never happened. Unverified underwater sounds—bangs, pings, imagined Morse code—were treated as life signs. Television networks aired countdown clocks as if the vessel were still intact and waiting to be rescued, even as experts privately suspected the sub had likely imploded shortly after contact was lost. One British tabloid splashed the headline "TRAPPED IN THE TITANIC TOMB" across its cover, reinforcing a grotesque fantasy.

This reaction was not just about risk—it was about wealth and status. When tragedy befalls the rich or famous, it triggers a special kind of fascination, tinged with schadenfreude. In an era of extreme inequality, the suffering of the privileged is often recast as cosmic justice. Social media supercharges this: Mockery spreads faster than compassion. The *Titan* passengers were quickly reduced to caricatures—tech bros, clueless billionaires, fools with too much money. Their humanity was stripped away in favor of a more clickable narrative. It was theater of the macabre, not journalism.

However, in the summer of 2023, journalism was on life support, and science journalism was on the brink of extinction.

For decades, the science beat was a vital part of the journalistic landscape. Reporters were encouraged to specialize, to develop fluency in fields like aerospace, climate, medicine, and engineering. But over the past twenty years, those roles have been slashed or dissolved entirely.

In 2008, CNN eliminated its robust, award-winning science unit, summarily dismissing seven science-savvy producers and reporters, and me.

Today, I am the last full-time science correspondent on US network television, and fewer than 3 percent of American reporters and editors are dedicated to covering science. These aren't just numbers; they represent the erosion of institutional knowledge, the hollowing out of specialization, and the rise of an era where the complex is oversimplified and the nuanced is overlooked.

Meanwhile, between 2008 and 2020, US newsroom employment fell by 26 percent, with journalism jobs dropping a staggering 57 percent. As newsrooms shrink and deadlines accelerate, the generalists who remain are stretched thin, and highly technical stories—like the *Titan* implosion—are viewed as real-life drama made for ratings and clicks.

But there was another factor at play here. OceanGate, the company behind *Titan*, offered no public statement in the crucial days after contact was lost. No spokesperson stepped up. No one provided context or credibility. Nature abhors a vacuum, and into that void rushed speculation. The CEO and pilot, Stockton Rush, was cast as a reckless thrill seeker. The passengers were mocked as clueless billionaires. The vessel's carbon-fiber hull became a symbol of hubris.

There are elements of truth in all of that. But the real story is more complicated.

I first met Stockton Rush in 2010, when I accepted his invitation to dive in *Antipodes*, a submersible that OceanGate had purchased and modified, to learn the ropes of undersea exploration. The dive took place in Puget Sound. The water clarity there is not great, so we didn't see much, but I saw enough to know this: Stockton wasn't a trust-funded dilettante. He was curious, driven, and sincerely motivated to open access to the deep ocean. He wasn't building toys. He was building tools for scientists, educators, and, yes, even journalists like me. He wanted to democratize deep-sea exploration, and as he piloted *Antipodes*, he appeared to know exactly what he was doing.

My invitation was facilitated by OceanGate co-founder Guillermo Söhnlein, whom I had met six years earlier, in 2004. At the time, Guillermo was running the International Association of Space Entrepreneurs. He was drawn to exploration and entrepreneurship, but what struck me was his mindset: methodical, systems oriented, linear in his thinking. He wasn't just chasing dreams—he was building the foundation of a nascent industry. Reading this book only reinforces my impression that Guillermo was exactly the kind of partner Stockton needed to help OceanGate push the envelope without tearing it.

I can't help but wonder how things might have transpired if he had remained at the helm. Maybe the tragedy could have been avoided. But even if it wasn't, I'm certain the story would have been told differently. Guillermo would have stepped up. He would have communicated. He would have filled the vacuum with facts, rather than leaving it to be filled with fiction.

As I often tell people, the demand for facts is inversely proportional to their availability. It does indeed take time for the real story to emerge from a maelstrom of tragedy. However, our attention spans often don't match that time frame, unfortunately.

This book, *Titan Unfinished*, is a valuable attempt to pull the signal from the noise. Guillermo Söhnlein writes not as an outsider, but as someone who helped build the company. He offers context, perspective, and a refusal to indulge in easy answers. He doesn't excuse every decision, but he resists the impulse to oversimplify.

The truth doesn't float to the surface. You must dive for it. And we should never consider that mission finished either.

Miles O'Brien

Science Correspondent, *PBS NewsHour*

Former Science Correspondent, CNN

PREFACE

FOR ONE WEEK DURING THE SUMMER OF 2023, THE ENTIRE WORLD WAS fixated on a single news story that captured every headline and every lead on every outlet: the search and rescue operation for the research submersible, *Titan*, and the ultimate tragic fate of its five crew members when it was finally discovered that the sub had imploded. The media frenzy was fueled by many captivating storylines, but its primary focus was the villain at the center of it all—namely, Richard Stockton Rush III, the vessel's pilot and designer, and the co-founder and CEO of OceanGate, the company that owned and operated the sub.

Stockton was my friend. He was also my co-founder at OceanGate. His story—and that of our ambitious venture—is *nothing* like how it has been portrayed in the media.

To fully understand the man and the company, you have to understand the journey, starting with the events that led to the founding of OceanGate and continuing through the fateful dive and beyond. For better or worse, I am one of the only people who has had a front-row seat to the entire story. Therefore, the moral obligation—or the historic privilege—of chronicling the tale falls to me.

Just to be clear, I did not want to write this book. I would have much preferred that no one died. I did not need the massive disruption in my life that this book has produced. I did not need people thinking that I was trying to profit financially from the death of my friend and the other four crew members. However, I felt that I had to write it.

My primary motivation is to ensure that anyone who forms an opinion regarding these events does so with a proper factual foundation and adequate context. I do not intend to defend Stockton as a flawless individual, OceanGate as a perfect venture, or *Titan* as an ideal of technology innovation, because they were none of these. However, I also know from personal experience that the media's characterizations of Stockton, OceanGate, and *Titan* are nowhere close to being accurate. The truth lies somewhere in the nuances between the two extremes, and this is where I hope to shine a brighter light.

I have been fortunate enough to have had a varied career that has spanned economics, law, military, entrepreneurship, venture investing, technology innovation, and philanthropy, all covering the fields of high technology, space, oceans, exploration, and sustainability. Along the way, I have met hundreds of talented, passionate, and disciplined individuals and worked with dozens of incredibly committed teams around the world. However, partnering with Stockton on our OceanGate venture was one of the most formative experiences of my life. I only hope that in the pages that follow, I can do justice to those memories and help readers truly appreciate the power of entrepreneurship and technology innovation when applied to a social mission aimed at improving life on Earth for all of humanity.

I served as co-founder, CEO, and board member of OceanGate from August 2009 to January 2013, and I retained a very small ownership stake even after leaving. I was not part of the company while it developed the *Titan* submersible or its predecessor *Cyclops*, and I never participated in any of the expeditions to the wreck of the *Titanic*. However, during the decade after my departure, I kept in touch with Stockton and occasionally visited the team, either at their offices or at one of their expedition sites. He and I never stopped viewing ourselves as co-founders.

Finally, in order to honor the legacies of the five lost crew members, I am donating proceeds from this book to charities that award grants to young explorers who embody the values of "exploration through innovation." I truly believe that only the passage of time will provide proper context for how to best view the events of the past fifteen years, so in the meantime I want to ensure that young explorers continue to learn from past victories and tragedies as they write their own chapters in the long-running epic of exploration.

This story is as old as humanity and will forever remain unfinished.

Guillermo A. M. Söhnlein
Barcelona, Spain
December 2024

AUTHOR'S NOTE

THIS BOOK IS WRITTEN AS A MEMOIR, PRIMARILY FOCUSED ON MY PERsonal interactions with Stockton Rush from the founding of OceanGate to just before his death. I am also including my own experiences with the tragic accident and the fallout since then.

As with all memoirs, this book boasts the power of my firsthand experience and suffers from the limitations of my singular perspective. By definition, these pages contain my memories and recollections, at least to the best that I can recall them after all these years. I have not fact-checked myself with others who may have shared these events, in large part because I know they are still grieving and coping with the loss. I only hope that I come close to being accurate, but any defects in this regard are purely my own fault.

I want to give readers an appreciation for Stockton as a person, so I try sharing some of the many conversations that he and I had over the years. Obviously, I cannot remember them verbatim, but there are many of his iconic statements that are etched indelibly into my brain. At a minimum, I believe I capture the general substance and sentiments of our talks.

One critical item I do *not* include in this book is my personal opinion on the cause of the fateful implosion. Since, as of this writing, the accident investigations are still ongoing and final reports have not yet been released, no one—myself included—has enough facts or evidence to determine a cause. Any attempt to do so is pure speculation, which is something that critics and the media have done enough of over the past months. I refuse to participate in this endeavor.

Chapter 1

VIENNA

June 19, 2023

Vienna, Austria

"TITANIC TOURIST SUBMERSIBLE GOES MISSING SPARKING SEARCH" WAS the headline on the SmartNews article link my girlfriend sent me on my European WhatsApp. I glanced at my phone while walking through the streets of Vienna with the team from the BOLD Community and my fellow speakers from the Exportagg 2023 conference, which was scheduled to begin the following morning. I instantly got a horrible feeling in the pit of my stomach.

Without reading the piece, I already knew what it would reveal. My friends were in big trouble, perhaps even dead. There was only one submersible—tourist or otherwise—with plans to dive on the wreck of the *Titanic* that summer.

Hoping against hope that I was wrong, I clicked on the link and read the article. Sadly, I was not wrong. And thus began one of the worst weeks of my life.

I had arrived in Vienna earlier that day for what I was anticipating to be an inspirational event, meeting innovative thinkers from around the world and speaking onstage about the virtues of space exploration to a non-space business audience. I had helped recruit two fellow space entrepreneurs for our panel discussion, and they were scheduled to arrive later in the evening. While I waited for them, I immersed myself in fascinating discussions with some of the other insightful speakers and with the dedicated team from the BOLD Community that had gathered us for the pre-conference dinner. We were treated to a beautiful, sunny afternoon walking tour of Vienna, and that is when I received the fateful news.

I had been to Vienna several times before, and it was (and still is) one of my favorite cities in the world. However, the rest of that evening became a blur, and I felt like I was floating through the streets in a haze. I could not focus or even think. I remember feeling like a zombie, physically alive but dead inside.

I tuned out all of the conversations that evening and lost myself in my phone, searching for any and all information regarding the evolving situation in the Atlantic Ocean. For better or worse, the incident was quickly garnering global media attention, so there seemed to be no shortage of data to scour through. Most of it was clearly clickbait or completely wild uninformed speculation, but with my industry experience I could filter through all of the noise and identify valuable nuggets that I could start piecing together into a proper narrative in my head.

I began feeling nauseous with the stark reality I was going to have to accept. My company's submersible had likely imploded, instantly killing all five crew members, including my co-founder and friend, Stockton Rush.

I felt alone, with no one to turn to.

I was at a business conference with a group of speakers selected for their success in entrepreneurship and technology innovation. Not many there were involved with ventures or projects that could potentially lead to fatalities. No one could empathize.

Then my two space colleagues arrived.

Both of them were space entrepreneurs with grand visions of helping humanity expand into the cosmos. They knew the risks involved with exploration of extreme environments, so they knew the very real potential for loss of life along that path. *They* could empathize.

For the rest of that evening and through the next two days of the conference, they were the pillars of strength that kept me going and, frankly, kept me from falling apart. I do not know how I could have made it through those first few days without them, and I will always owe them a debt of gratitude I cannot possibly repay.

The media reports stated that *Titan* had lost communications with its surface support ship at some point on Sunday, June 18, a full twenty-four hours before I learned of their situation. Everyone seemed focused on the ninety-six hours of emergency life support aboard the sub and on the rapidly escalating search and rescue effort on the open ocean. I let myself play out the various scenarios in my head, imagining what Stockton and the crew might be doing or how the surface support crew would be faring.

At one point, I finally managed to get a call through to my friend who also served on OceanGate's board of directors. Even though the board members were in constant contact with the crew on the support ship, he did not have much more information for me. Like everyone else, we were all hoping that the five crew members were still safely inside the sub and that they would be rescued before their life support was exhausted.

However, deep inside I knew they were likely already gone.

Watching from a distance and reading between the lines of media reports, some things just did not add up. The most troubling issue was that the support ship could not locate the sub. I had never dived in *Titan*, and I was never part of our expeditions to the *Titanic*, but I knew that our subs carried tracking beacons so the surface crew would always know where we were. Those beacons were powered by systems that were completely independent from the underwater radios, so it would require multiple simultaneous failures to lose both at the same time. In fact, the only unlikely scenario I could think of where this would occur was the one I feared the most: implosion.

I have very little recollection of the two panel discussions I participated in during the conference. My mind was dulled by the events unfolding a quarter of a world away, and I could not think of anything else. I do not know if I even slept the rest of my time in Vienna. By Wednesday, I somehow managed to get myself on a flight back to my Airbnb in Barcelona, the city to which I was in the process of relocating. By Thursday morning, with the ninety-six-hour life support deadline looming and still with no sign of the sub, I slogged my way to the Barcelona airport to pick up my girlfriend, who had already been scheduled for weeks to take a red-eye from the United States to visit me for the coming weekend. I practically collapsed in her arms.

A few hours later, the two of us watched live on my laptop as the US Coast Guard officer in charge of the search and rescue operation held a press conference and made the announcement I knew was coming: *Titan* had, in fact, imploded, instantly killing all five members of the crew.

My friend was gone forever.

Chapter 2

RICHARD STOCKTON RUSH III

June 2009
Monterey, California

"YOU MUST BE STOCKTON," I SAID. "IT'S GREAT TO FINALLY MEET YOU IN person."

I reached out to shake his hand, but instead he presented his elbow for what I would later learn was his preferred greeting, long before COVID-19 forced everyone into similar elbow bumps. Even though he and I had already exchanged several emails and talked on conference calls, it was nice to finally connect a face to the voice.

He was in his mid-forties, just three years older than me, and of medium height and build, just like me, but our similarities ended there. His salt-and-pepper hair, piercing blue eyes, flashing smile, and clean-cut appearance gave him what most people would call "boyish good looks." He was as charismatic and energetic in person as he was on the phone.

We were on a pier in Monterey Bay, with me heading off to the airport for a flight back to my home in Northern Virginia and him just arriving from his home in Seattle for a day of discussions about submersible designs with the team I had just left at the other end of the pier. The entire exchange lasted no more than sixty seconds, but somehow I could not shake the feeling that my life had just changed forever.

Graham Hawkes was the man leading the sub team that day. He was the one I had been working with and the one Stockton had come to meet with. He was the one who brought the two of us together, so it would be fair to say that OceanGate would not have happened without him.

Graham was a well-known longtime submersible designer, who had pioneered the use of carbon fiber as a key material for deep-diving pressure hulls. He also had the novel idea of using inverted wings to build submersibles that would "fly" underwater, which is why his technology company was called DeepFlight. I was introduced to him in 2008 via my finance startup, Space Angels Network, where he had applied for seed funding into his fledgling underwater tourism venture, Ocean Galactic. Even though I had never even heard of submersibles, I was instantly captivated by Graham's "flying sub" designs and spent several months crossing the country from my home in Northern Virginia to his home in the San Francisco Bay Area to help support his business efforts on a consulting basis.

This is how I first heard of Stockton Rush.

I do not remember how Stockton found Graham, but I know that he wanted to help finance the initial build of Graham's

DeepFlight 2 carbon fiber submersible. The two of them had negotiated an agreement, and Graham asked me to review it for any potential problems. I really did not find any, but this transaction was my initial contact with Stockton.

Through all of those early interactions with him on Graham's behalf, whether via document exchanges, emails, or phone calls, I found him to be extremely knowledgeable about both engineering and business. He seemed reasonable and flexible. Even better, during conference calls he came across as intense but extremely funny. It is the only way I can think of describing his unique mix of energy and sense of humor.

Through those early interactions, he and I discovered that we shared a few common interests, and that bond would continue to grow over the coming weeks, months, and years.

We were both frustrated astronauts who had grown up inspired by Captain Kirk with dreams of exploring the solar system but had been stymied in our pursuit of joining NASA because of our poor eyesight. We had each taken different paths through our careers, with him focusing on becoming an engineer and a pilot, while I went to law school and served in the Marine Corps. We found common ground in our love of innovative startups, me as a serial entrepreneur and him as an angel investor.

I quickly grew to trust him, and even to like him.

As my business relationship with Graham evolved, I conceived of an idea for a new venture that he and I could co-found. I would serve as CEO and he would serve as CTO, and our business model would be to mass-produce and sell all of his various innovative "winged submersible" designs as product lines for different uses and target customers. I started crafting the business pitch deck, because we would likely have to raise $2 million to $3 million from seed investors.

Meanwhile, he and Stockton continued to grow their partnership working on *DeepFlight 2*. Over time, it became clear that Stockton was looking to be a passive investor in a submersible venture but wanted someone other than Graham to run it, so Graham would be free to focus 100 percent of his energy and talents on technology designs.

During the summer of 2009, Graham and the team from DeepFlight were scheduled to spend a few weeks in Monterey Bay conducting sea trials of his *Super Falcon 2* carbon fiber shallow-diving winged submersible. I agreed to be there for a week, and Stockton agreed to come down from Seattle. It would be the best opportunity for us to meet face-to-face to explore if there was a possibility of all three of us somehow working together. Unfortunately, our respective travel plans allowed only the momentary overlap on the pier, but it was enough.

Stockton and I hit it off right away, and thus began a partnership and friendship that lasted until his death fourteen years later.

Chapter 3

MEDIA FRENZY

June 2023
Barcelona, Spain

I COULD NOT BELIEVE THE MEDIA COVERAGE. IT WAS EVERYWHERE. MAINSTREAM, online, social media, radio, TV. Every country and every language, it seemed. Journalists, podcasters, YouTubers, politicians, CEOs, celebrities . . . everyone was talking about it, and very publicly, too. I could not remember the last time I had seen such widespread attention on a story that did not have global ramifications, like a military conflict, a pandemic, an economic crisis, or a US presidential election involving Donald Trump. Maybe when Queen Elizabeth died? Definitely when Princess Diana died. This was insane.

It was surreal to me that all of this commotion was about my company. And my friend.

Why did so many people care about a small sub in the middle

of the Atlantic? Why was there so much attention on the plight of five individuals? Someone mentioned that there was nowhere near this much focus drawn to the plight of 300 refugees who had drowned recently trying to reach Europe from Africa. Some thought it reeked of racism or elitism. I hoped it was something more profound.

For four days, the world was fixated on the expansive search and rescue operations racing against the clock to find the crew before their emergency life support ran out. It was an Apollo 13 moment, and it captivated audiences across the globe.

As everyone struggled to quickly become experts in the very tiny niche world of crewed submersibles, several narratives began to emerge. I believe the international phenomenon was due to three overlapping Venn diagram circles, with one key element thrown in as the kicker.

First, this was a story about exploration. I believe that humans are explorers by nature. Even if someone does not have any particular interest in exploring themselves, they are still fascinated by others who risk their lives to go places no one has ever gone before. Of course, a dive to the wreck of the *Titanic* is not really "exploration" per se, since dozens of people have visited that grave site. However, plunging 3,800 meters (12,500 feet) into the dark depths of the ocean is something that has been done by far fewer than 1,000 of the 100 billion *Homo sapiens* who have ever lived on this planet. This is precisely the kind of extraordinary story that captures people's imaginations.

Second, this was a story about rich people. Granted, for some, this was a turnoff. However, for most, this was a fascination. Despite the negative feelings many people have toward the uberwealthy, they are still curious about how those people lead their privileged lives. Whether it is through the tabloids and paparazzi, in-depth behind-the-scenes interviews, social media posts, autobiographies, or myriad other means, the general public always seems to want to know details about the lives of the "1 percent." The fact that two of the *Titan* crew members were allegedly billionaires, one was the son of a billionaire, and one was a multimillionaire, provided the juicy fodder for mass media audiences and, of course, for the vast social media crowd.

Third, this was a story about technology innovation and entrepreneurship. Since the dawn of the Industrial Revolution, humanity's use of technology has expanded at an exponential rate. Researchers and inventors seem to come up with new creative ways to improve our lives on an almost daily basis, and then entrepreneurs and investors commercialize them and bring them to market. We are living through an almost sci-fi-esque *technology revolution* that is spreading to virtually every part of the world. Each new breakthrough is newsworthy, and we naturally tend to celebrate—if not idolize or even worship—those visionary individuals who overcome all odds to think outside the box. Apple famously called them "the crazy ones" in arguably its most successful marketing campaign.

Which leads to the extra "kicker" for this particular story: a villain named Stockton Rush.

Over the course of those first four days, it seemed like every storyline that broke was something negative about Stockton. He was a charismatic con man who bilked rich people out of millions. He was a wannabe Elon Musk who did not have his idol's technical skills or business acumen. He was a self-styled maverick who wanted to innovate just for the sake of innovating. He was a rule-breaker who completely disregarded every accepted norm for safety and ignored every warning issued by professionals with much greater experience and credentials. He was a stubborn, thin-skinned tyrant who fired anyone who disagreed with him and viciously attacked those who tried to stop him. He was a spoiled rich kid who ironically ran a cheap operation and cut corners to save money. The worst one was that he was a distraught individual with mental issues who had carefully orchestrated a high-profile murder-suicide of rich people to secure his place in the storied legacy of his family's proud heritage.

Honestly, I would not have minded the onslaught but for the fact that I could not reconcile any of it with the Stockton Rush that I knew. While there were kernels of truth behind every allegation, the conclusions drawn by the critics and the unwitting journalists were either off-target misinterpretations, outlandish exaggerations, or flat-out wrong conclusions.

As this unfolded in real time, I could not believe that everyone was falling for it.

Thinking objectively, even if I had not known Stockton, I would have been immediately suspicious of any story that was so incredibly one-sided. As I watched, read, and listened to the media coverage, I found myself yelling at no one and everyone, "Are you telling me that you could not find a single person on this planet to say a single good thing about this guy? And you expect us to buy this?"

Yet the firestorm was nonstop. It seemed to feed on itself, with each journalist trying to outdo the others by uncovering even more garbage about the man allegedly responsible for the first submersible fatalities in almost half a century.

However, I could not entirely blame the media. They were just doing their jobs. They were trying like crazy to work as quickly as possible to learn about the submersible community, OceanGate, *Titan*, the *Titanic* expeditions, and, of course, Stockton Rush. All while simultaneously covering the rapidly evolving search and rescue operation taking place on the open ocean in the middle of the Atlantic. Also, they had to understand what their audiences wanted to see, hear, and read, while their bosses had to keep in mind how the outlet made money. Again, everyone was simply doing their jobs and doing them frighteningly well.

The problem that I saw—and the frustration that I felt—was that there appeared to be no one from OceanGate speaking publicly about anything. I figured that they were remaining silent under the advice of their lawyers and PR firms, but if that was the case, then I completely disagreed with that advice.

As a CEO and as a board member at various other ventures, I was always taught that the number one rule of crisis management was to take charge of the narrative. I could not understand why the company did not put a spokesperson in front of cameras and microphones immediately. Initially, I thought for sure that we would hear from a member of the management team, or a board member, or a representative from the PR team. Something, anything, if even just to say, "Everyone is focused on trying to get our friends and colleagues back safely; our thoughts are with them and their families, and we will answer questions after their return."

Instead, the only people speaking to the media were the experts who had been critics of Stockton and OceanGate almost from the beginning. They all came out of the woodwork to provide their two cents' worth. Even James Cameron weighed in. It was such a wild lopsided affair.

But again, I did not begrudge any of these people either. I knew each of them personally (except for Cameron), and I knew they were certainly qualified to provide their opinions as industry experts (including, and especially, Cameron). Most of them had their own businesses to protect, so they had to quickly distance themselves from the escalating narrative around OceanGate and highlight the differences that might preserve their reputations for safety. I was sure that their lawyers and PR firms had advised them to go on the offensive in order to avoid getting painted with the same brush as that villain Stockton.

That said, I was angered by two issues.

First, even in the midst of the search and rescue operation, everyone was speculating on what had happened. And it was precisely that: *speculation*.

The experts who were educating the media and hence the general public did not have a shred of evidence or verified information to work with, and yet they were speaking confidently and eloquently on what had happened. They blamed the use of carbon fiber for the hull, the cylindrical shape of the hull, the supposed lack of testing, the refusal to get a certificate from a classification agency on a new sub design, the launch and retrieval platform, the towing operation—the list went on and on.

The most frustrating for me was James Cameron, who was, in my opinion, the most qualified expert to appear on camera. Most people who know him only for his movies do not realize that he is an accomplished ocean explorer and sub designer, as well as a sub pilot who will always hold the record for being the first human to dive solo to the deepest part of the ocean. However, as far as I knew, he had never seen *Titan*'s designs, test data, and dive or maintenance logs; he had never visited the facilities, dived in the sub, or even seen the sub; and he had never met Stockton or spoken with him. Talk about pure speculation! Amazingly, the media ate it up, most likely because he was, well, James Cameron. At least most of the other experts had some working knowledge of *Titan* and knew Stockton, primarily because he had spent so many years trying to get them to help OceanGate with the development of this new sub.

Regardless, one thing was true for everyone: Until the sub was found and an investigation was completed, they were all just speculating. It would take months, if not years, before anyone could have a meaningful discussion about the potential cause of the implosion.

I should pause here to highlight one notable exception. Richard Garriott was the president of The Explorers Club, arguably the most well-respected and well-established organization of explorers in the world. He has personally flown in space, dived to the bottom of the Mariana Trench and to the wreck of the *Titanic*, and stood at the North and South Poles, among many other extraordinary accomplishments. Two of the *Titan* crew members, Hamish Harding and PH Nargeolet, were members of The Explorers Club, and Stockton had given several talks at their New York City headquarters.

I do not know how Richard felt about Stockton, OceanGate, or *Titan*, so I do not know if he shared the critics' concerns about any of the safety risks. However, what I do know is that he immediately recognized his responsibility to his 3,000-plus members, the crew, and the global community, so he quickly sprang into action, calling publicly and privately to marshal whatever resources were needed to support the search and rescue operations in the Atlantic. I do not recall if he said these words exactly, but my memory is that he took the general approach of saying, "Look, there will be a time and place to determine what went wrong and to assign blame, if any, but right now we need to all pull together to get our friends and colleagues back safely." I remember being proud of having been a member of The Explorers Club and honored to know Richard personally.

Despite that single bright light, the second issue that angered me about the many talking heads speaking with the media was that I truly believe that the approach each one took was *not* the approach Stockton would have taken had the tables been reversed.

Yes, he would have gone in front of cameras to distance OceanGate's model from theirs. He might have even given in to the temptation to speculate on what had happened. However, I am absolutely convinced that he would not have spoken derisively about anyone or about anyone else's business, technology, or operations. Despite his strong opinions and heated differences with others in the community, he would have been respectful and professional, biting his tongue during media interviews. In private, he probably would have let loose, but not in public. He appreciated too well that the global ocean exploration community was too small and its shared mission too important for anyone in the general public to think negatively about any of its members.

Every time I watched someone cut into Stockton in the media, I imagined what he would have said under inverse circumstances:

Ocean exploration is a difficult, risky business, especially in the deep ocean. Those of us that do this for a living have a healthy respect for that risk, and we do it anyway. Why? Mostly to help push humanity forward and improve life here on Earth, but also because exploration is in our DNA. That also requires us to push the envelope on technology and think outside the box. [Insert name of the sub designer/operator/explorer who was in danger] is one of these pioneers, and I'm proud to consider them a fellow explorer and innovator. I may not see eye-to-eye with them on how to build and operate subs, but then again it's precisely that kind of diversity of thought that has always led to advances in science and innovation. I hope that they and the rest of the crew get back safely to their friends, families, and colleagues, and I look forward to discussing with them any lessons they learned from this experience so that the rest of our sub community can benefit.

Or something to that effect.

Knowing Stockton as I did, I could certainly see and hear him making these kinds of public statements. It made me sad to see that this was not the path others chose. Then it made me mad that this approach resulted in Stockton being depicted in the media the way he was.

I felt helpless, and I was desperate to do something about it. But what?

As the days passed and the vicious rhetoric escalated, I wanted so badly to jump into the fray. I certainly had plenty of opportunities, because my phones, emails, and social media had been lighting up with countless requests for interviews from journalists aggressively seeking public comments from anyone who knew Stockton personally. They were getting stonewalled by the company, so they were tracking down everyone who used to work at OceanGate, but they were all either in shock, grieving, or unwilling to get attacked publicly. As Stockton's co-founder, I seemed to be their top choice, even though I had not been at the company in over a decade.

I knew that if I wanted to, I could pop up my head and instantly have a global megaphone with which to try correcting all of the inaccuracies that were being spread. It would be a fool's errand, because the momentum was so strong that there was no realistic hope of stemming the negative tide. I had had enough experience with the media to understand that, at best, all I would get is a few soundbites with which to push some points across. I also knew that I would get skewered by severe backlash for appearing to defend such a villainous person as Stockton.

Besides, while I disagreed with the advice the company had been receiving from its lawyers and PR firm, I wanted to respect their professional opinions and not sabotage whatever progress they felt they were making with their "stay quiet" strategy. I was still a minority shareholder, and I had to trust the board to do the right thing.

More importantly, as petty as this felt given the dire circumstances, I really could not afford such a huge distraction in my life. I was in the process of launching a couple of new ventures, and I was on the boards of three nonprofit organizations. I did not want to bring any negative publicity to those efforts, and I needed to stay focused on my work for them. On a personal note, just two weeks before the accident, I had moved from Atlanta to Barcelona, and I had a slog of a relocation process ahead of me. Also, I did not want to expose my three grown children to the public attacks I was certain would be leveled against me.

All of my friends and colleagues reached out to check on me, but also to ensure that I would not do anything stupid like make myself available to the media. I received the same messages from friends who were lawyers, PR professionals, CEOs, board members, life coaches, and, well, everyone.

"Keep your head down."

"Fight the urge to talk, because nothing good will come of it."

"Think of your own career and your own family."

I knew they were right. And yet for three days, I struggled with the guilt of standing by while I watched my friend getting publicly persecuted. I waited for the company to come to his defense. I waited for the news cycle to shift. I waited for someone other than me to jump into the mix and provide a coherent alternative perspective. No one did.

The entire time I had Stockton's voice in my head. I wondered what he would do if the roles had been reversed and if I had been the one subjected to such pervasive vitriol.

I knew the answer. I just had to get comfortable accepting it.

Chapter 4

FOUNDING OCEANGATE

August 2009
British Columbia, Canada

I HAD NEVER SNAPPED THE HEAD OFF A LIVE SHRIMP BEFORE, BUT THERE were dozens to prepare, and clearly Stockton needed help.

We were floating in a small power boat north of Vancouver, and he had just brought up several traps that he had left out overnight. He showed us how to take off a shrimp's head, toss it overboard, and drop the body into the waiting bucket at our feet, so we could later take the lot of them to the house and boil them for dinner. Neither Graham nor his wife wanted to participate in this part of the meal. Honestly, I did not relish the idea either, but I wanted to help speed the process along.

Stockton had invited the three of us to join him for a weekend "off-site" at his second home. During those two days, we got to know each other better and brainstormed high-level business ideas—and ultimately decided to start a company called Deep-Flight Technologies and made plans for potential next steps.

We agreed to generally follow my original idea to commercialize and mass-produce Graham's various winged sub designs. In many ways, it was going to be a perfect three-way partnership, with Graham providing the technical expertise and the intellectual property from his prior sub designs, Stockton providing the seed capital and board oversight, and me providing operational leadership as CEO.

Since Stockton was contributing the startup capital and was busy with multiple time commitments that limited his travel, he insisted that we base our new company near his home in Seattle. Graham and his wife knew it would be difficult for their two kids to move from the San Francisco Bay Area, but they seemed generally open to the idea. I had to call my then-wife, Julie, back home in Virginia, and she reluctantly agreed, knowing that the burden of the cross-country relocation would likely fall on her shoulders and that our three kids would have a difficult transition.

I knew that moving across the country to jump into a new startup was an absolutely crazy idea, even under the most ideal circumstances. However, to make this particular idea completely insane, that weekend was the only other time I had ever seen Stockton in person since our initial brief encounter in Monterey. Every neuron in my brain was firing warning signals, but every fiber in my gut told me it was the right thing to do. At that point, I had been an entrepreneur for over a decade, so I had learned to trust my instincts. Something inside told me that opportunity had not only knocked but had also opened a door for me. I felt compelled to step through it.

By the end of the weekend, the four of us made a verbal commitment to launch the new venture right away. We shook hands, and I started the process of relocating my family from the East Coast to the Pacific Northwest.

August 2009
Seattle, Washington

FROM 5,000 FEET, THE GREEN PASTURES BELOW SEEMED QUIET AND PEACEful. I did not realize that there were open spaces like this just north of downtown Seattle. I was impressed with how quickly the 300-horsepower two-seat Glasair III had flown us in the wide circle around the whole city. As Stockton promised, it was a nice aerial tour of what was soon to become the new hometown for me and my family.

We hit a pocket of bad air, and the whole plane shook quite violently. I did not want to let any nerves show, so I kept my gaze fixed on the ground below, only allowing myself a side glance at the right wing fluttering just a few feet outside the cockpit.

It suddenly dawned on me that agreeing to this impromptu sightseeing flight might not have been such a great idea. After all, I had just met Stockton a few weeks prior and had not spent much time getting to know him. We clicked right away because we seemed to agree philosophically on how to best approach new venture creation and technology innovation. However, deciding to co-found a startup was a much different endeavor than trusting my life to his aerospace engineering and piloting skills.

The plane we were flying was a kit that he had built himself—well, more like assembled—a few years before. I had not done any research into the company that sold him the kit, nor had I questioned him much on his ability to put together such a plane safely. As we shook again in more rough air, I doubted my instinct to trust him implicitly.

I also knew that he had been flying since he was a teenager and had many hours of experience, but that did not necessarily mean that he was a good pilot. After all, I complained every day about terrible drivers on the road, even though I was sure all of them had valid licenses and more than enough experience. I thought perhaps I should have inquired a bit more before embarking on this little adventure.

While my mind was preoccupied with the potentially unsafe situation I might be in, I heard Stockton's voice in my headset.

"Wanna do a barrel roll?" he asked.

I thought he was kidding, so without taking my gaze off the ground below, I replied flatly, "Sure. Why not?"

Before I finished my sentence, I felt the plane suddenly slide out from under me to my left. I swung my head around to look ahead through the front windshield, only to see the horizon inverted, with the blue sky below the green pastures. My mind could not grasp what was happening, but instantly we were back to flight level. Had I just completed my first barrel roll?

I looked at him and yelled into the microphone, "What the hell was that?"

He just laughed and calmly replied, "You said you wanted to do a barrel roll."

"I thought you were kidding!"

"Relax. This plane was designed for aerobatics, and I have an aerobatics license. Unfortunately, none of my friends will ever let me do any stunts with them, and honestly it's not that fun by yourself." He seemed genuinely dejected.

For some reason, in my head, this changed everything. It was almost like I had been questioning the car and the driver, but now he had just told me that the car was designed by a Formula 1 team and he had been an F1 driver. I felt my mind conduct an instantaneous risk-reward analysis, and then my comfort level flipped completely.

"Well, I'm in! What else can you do?"

We spent the next ten minutes doing more barrel rolls, as well as high-G turns, loops, and even some parabolas, where Stockton gave me his watch to hold in the palm of my hand so I could observe it floating during the microgravity portion of the flight profile. Those were ten of the most exhilarating minutes of my life!

Suddenly, as quickly as it had started, it was over.

"Why'd you stop?" I complained.

"I have to. I'm getting a bit nauseous."

I was crestfallen, realizing that my joyride was over. However, in that moment, I fully appreciated my new co-founder on a number of levels.

First, I recognized that I could easily trust the airplane and the pilot during any turbulence. That part was a given.

More importantly, I felt a deep sense of comfort with Stockton as an engineer and as a pilot. He was certainly confident and seemed completely competent, at least as far as I could assess, given that I was neither an engineer nor a pilot. However, he also demonstrated a healthy respect for risk, a commitment to safety, and an emotionally mature self-recognition of his own limits. Moments earlier I had been hesitant to show my nerves in front of him, but then he had had no qualms about admitting his own weaknesses in front of me.

I knew right then that I could trust him with my life.

September 2009

Everett, Washington

WE STOOD INSIDE THE HUGE EMPTY AIRPLANE HANGAR—THE HOME FOR our new business venture. I still could not believe that Stockton would go to such lengths in order to appease Graham. His rationale certainly made sense, but I had never seen an investor/co-founder bend over backward this much for one of his fellow co-founders.

Stockton knew that Graham was going to be the technical genius behind our new venture, and he appreciated that Graham and his wife were going to have to uproot their family of two school-age kids from their lives in California to embark on this adventure in Seattle. It was really the only firm request Stockton had made in exchange for putting up all of the seed funding. After all, he had family commitments of his own, and he did not want to be away from them by constantly commuting down to the Bay Area. Rather than taking a draconian approach of saying, "If you want my money, then you'll have to do things my way," he acknowledged Graham's sacrifice and tried to make it up to him in many ways.

The most obvious was our new hangar at Paine Field, where we would have offices and plenty of work space for Graham's team of engineers.

Why would a submersible company want to be based in an airplane hangar? Well, this is where Stockton's business rationale came in.

Our new venture would be called DeepFlight Technologies and would leverage Graham's unconventional approach of using inverted airplane wings to create the downward force allowing his subs to dive. This is why his subs looked more like fighter jets than any traditional underwater vessel. So there was definitely a branding rationale for choosing a hangar, as well as a corporate culture angle.

However, Stockton's primary reason for this choice was simple: He wanted Graham to be happy.

As an aerospace engineer with a lifelong passion for flight, Graham had spent years developing new submersible technologies. He was extremely proud of his new sub design approach, because it finally married his twin passions for flight and diving. It was his defining contribution to the global sub community, to the ocean exploration community, and to humanity itself. In many ways, this new line of flying subs would be the crowning achievement of his career and would cement his legacy as an industry innovator.

Stockton knew this, and he wanted to show Graham that he truly appreciated his immense talents. In a very real way, the hangar was Stockton's "welcome aboard" gift to his new co-founder.

For my part, I had already committed to relocating my family to Seattle. Julie was still in Virginia, selling our house and getting our household goods ready for the moving company while also taking care of the kids and their schooling. I had driven my car cross-country and settled into a long-term hotel to get the new company started while also conducting a search for our next home. In a few weeks, I would fly out to the East Coast and then drive the family back across to Seattle in our minivan.

Stockton and I left the hangar and drove to a nearby restaurant for lunch. We had a lot of business planning to discuss, but we were also still getting to know each other. Our conversations still drifted into our professional and personal histories, our views on current events, and general topics like politics, economics, religion, and so on. We also talked a lot about our families.

I found that Stockton's personality drove him to do almost everything extremely fast. He was highly intelligent, and his mind raced at breakneck speed, often jumping quickly from one topic to the next, making it difficult for anyone, including me, to keep up. As a huge fan of the television series *West Wing*, I used to joke that Stockton was a real-life Aaron Sorkin character, prone to intellectual rapid-fire dialogue. On more than one occasion, I would catch myself in a "walk and talk" conversation with him and would grin while laughing hysterically in my mind.

From our earliest conversations, he and I had bonded over being "frustrated astronauts," even though we were driven by a passion stronger than simply going to space. We both had Captain Kirk and Jacques Cousteau as our childhood heroes, and it was not until later in life that we each realized what those two had in common. It was their thirst for exploration. Going places no one had ever gone before, not just for adventure but for the potential of scientific discovery. It took us both until 2008 to realize that we could fulfill that urge for exploration and discovery right here on Earth. All we had to do was dive in a submersible.

By that point in my career, I had dealt with enough high-net-worth individuals to know that each of them had a unique story of how they accumulated their wealth. I had learned to engage them in conversations and let them share their own narrative, at the time, pace, and manner they wanted. Americans are fascinated by money but consider it a taboo topic for direct discussions. Instead, it has to flow naturally.

As he drove us to the restaurant, I wanted to learn more about him. “Since I’m moving to Seattle from Virginia and Graham is moving to Seattle from San Francisco, I’ve got to ask—why did you leave the Bay Area for Seattle however many years ago?”

“Mostly because I didn’t like the life that was expected of me there,” he started. “I came from a well-established family that was basically very high society. Lots of expectations. Lots of structure. Lots of rules. I wanted to live my own life. I wanted to have kids and not have to name my firstborn son Richard Stockton Rush IV just because I was Richard Stockton Rush III. I didn’t want to burden him with that same legacy I had to endure.”

“Isn’t he Ben?”

“Richard Benjamin Rush,” he said. “We actually had to get permission from the Benjamin Rush side of the family to call him Ben. Can you believe that?”

“What’s the Benjamin Rush side of the family?”

“He was one of the signers of the Declaration of Independence,” he explained. “Another was Richard Stockton. Benjamin married

Richard's daughter, Julia Stockton, so she became Julia Stockton Rush. One of their sons was called Richard Rush, who ended up being US attorney general, secretary of the treasury, and ambassador to England. These were some of my ancestors. Essentially, now there are a couple of family lines, and each one tries preserving their legacies in part through naming their sons. That's why I'm Richard Stockton Rush III."

He was not bragging nor was he trying to impress me. He was simply reciting his lineage, almost as if he had had it drilled into him from childhood. I was intellectually fascinated but not necessarily awestruck. After all, by then I had been fortunate enough to meet many incredible people, so I was somewhat jaded. Besides, his accomplished ancestors had been dead for over two centuries.

"Sounds cool, but also a pain," I said.

"No kidding! We actually have a collection of silhouette etchings tracing the family tree all the way back. It's kind of an heirloom. Each generation we trade back and forth the responsibility for taking care of it. I've got it now, but I can't wait to give it back."

I had always thought that being a descendant of famous ancestors would be a double-edged sword. Then again, I had also studied enough US history to know that many of the signers of the Declaration of Independence had died penniless. Just because one or two of Stockton's ancestors had been successful did not necessarily mean that they had created such vast generational wealth to survive into the modern day.

"So why was your life in San Francisco so bad?" I asked.

"Well, I wouldn't say it was bad," he replied. "It was just not what I wanted. I mean, my grandfather worked with J. Paul Getty, and my grandmother was Louise Davies."

"You mean from Davies Symphony Hall in SF?" I interrupted. During my law school days, I had seen performances there but had never bothered to research the namesake of the building.

"That's her. Like I said, not a bad life at all. It just wasn't the life I wanted."

Having grown up and gone to school in the Bay Area, I had heard long tales about the San Francisco high-society elites. The city's blue-blooded heritage traces its origins back to the gold rush era of the late nineteenth century, even before California became a state. The wealthiest were the railroad barons who made their fortunes selling support equipment to the entrepreneurial prospectors and opening up the West to the rest of the country. Names like Stanford, Huntington, Hopkins, and Crocker fill the pages of our state's history books. They established a long tradition for the highest echelons of San Francisco society.

I always wondered if it would be a good thing or a bad thing to be a part of that world. I knew it would not make me happy, so I was not surprised that Stockton felt the same.

We arrived at the restaurant and parked the car. As we walked in, I could not help but continue the conversation. After all, he still had not answered my initial question. "So, why Seattle?"

"This is one place in the country where you have a ton of rich people who don't care about being rich and don't want anyone to know they're rich. Everyone is down-to-earth. Unpretentious. You can have someone pull up in a Subaru and get out wearing jeans and boots, and you wouldn't know that they're a billionaire. They just don't care about all of the high-society crap that comes with wealth. For me, it was exactly where I wanted to be."

Actually, I had heard this about Seattle from other people over the years. As the hostess walked us through the restaurant to our booth, I looked around at everyone already seated and silently wondered how many of them were billionaires.

"Do you get back to the Bay Area much?" I asked once we had placed our food order.

"Every now and then. Mostly for the Bohemian Club."

"You're a Bohemian?"

"You know about the Bohemian Club?" he asked, surprised.

"Yeah. Well, sort of," I answered. "When I was at Cal, one of our fraternity alums was a member. Every year after the Big Game, he would host a group of us there. I got to meet quite a few members. All great guys. But they didn't tell me much about the club. I did a little research on my own. Highly exclusive, long waiting list, men only, lots of big names."

"You pretty much got it. I think the waitlist now is something like twenty-five years. It's crazy. And there are some huge names. You may not see them around the club much, but they all show up every year at the Grove."

"The Grove?" I asked. I had heard about this place, but I had never spoken with any member about it.

"The Bohemian Grove. It's the club's campground in Marin. Every summer we get most of the members to show up for a couple of weeks. We take turns giving a series of talks and performing for each other."

"Performing?"

"Well, that's why it's called the *Bohemian* Club. Our main mission is to support the arts. So there are two types of members: business members and artists. However, to really show support, each of the nonartist members at some point has to perform something.

Most guys end up joining skits or plays drawn up by the members who are writers."

This all sounded familiar from stories I had heard and some limited research I had done back while in college. I had always been torn on how to feel about it. On the one hand, it was commendable that people with financial resources were willing to support struggling artists. On the other hand, it felt so elitist. At least performing alongside the artists sounded like they were making an effort to treat them well.

"So what's your skill?" I asked.

"Stand-up comedy."

I almost spewed some of my Coke out my nostrils. If there was one thing I had already learned about Stockton, it was that he was an extremely private person. Not shy, just private. He really did not like drawing attention to himself, so I could not envision him onstage with all eyes on him. "What?"

"Yup. I just get up and tell jokes for twenty or thirty minutes."

I considered this for a moment. "I could see that. You're really good at telling jokes."

Stockton was an extremely talented joke-teller. Anyone who knew him or worked with him would say that it was one of his defining characteristics.

"That's also why I don't like repeating jokes. I'm always trying to come up with new material."

"Oh, yeah. I already noticed that. But it's kinda frustrating for the rest of us. I mean, we love it when you tell jokes. That's why we always ask you to tell us our favorites."

"Never gonna happen. I'm never going to repeat a joke. It's the sign of a lazy mind to keep relying on old material."

"C'mon. How many times do you think Abbott and Costello had to do their 'Who's on First?' routine? In fact, I read an interview with Chris Rock, who said that most people don't realize how scripted, preplanned, and rehearsed stand-up comedy really is."

"Maybe. But not me."

"So, you're like Robin Williams? He's the only one I can think of who never repeats a joke."

"Sure, let's go with that," he replied.

Months later, during a break in dive operations off the coast of Catalina Island in Southern California, our team was sitting around on the boat talking about Discovery Channel's idea of creating a reality TV series around OceanGate. This led to a game where everyone had to say which actor they would like to play them in a feature film about OceanGate. It was a fascinating psychological experiment to see how we viewed ourselves versus how the rest of the team viewed us.

When it was Stockton's turn, he said, "Richard Gere."

Everyone nodded quietly. Good-looking guy with salt-and-pepper hair. Like Gere's character in *Pretty Woman,* Stockton was a wealthy guy who invested in companies and struggled to live up to a powerful father. We could see why he would pick that particular actor. However, it was not the team's first choice for Stockton.

"You don't seem to agree," he said, weighing our stares.

There was clear hesitation on how to reply. After all, Stockton was ultimately our boss. It took a while before one of the sub pilots said quietly, "Well, Richard Gere wouldn't have been our first choice for you."

"Who then?"

"Jerry Seinfeld."

I was sitting next to Stockton, and I could feel him tense up, even as the group burst into laughter. "What?" he exclaimed.

I turned to him and tried to ease the tension. "Why not? He's one of the most successful comedians around. It's a huge compliment."

But he was not happy.

Back at our lunch, we finished eating and got into his car to return to the hangar. I was still curious about Seattle.

"So how do Wendy and the kids like it here?" I asked.

"They seem to like it. We've been here long enough. They've got their own lives here. Plus we have our place in Canada."

"The one where we met this summer?" Honestly, back then I had been so focused on our discussions with Graham about launching the new business that I had not really paid much attention to the house where we stayed.

"Yeah. Well, we're still finishing it. As you know, it's fairly remote and on the water. We have our own water, power, everything. Completely off-grid and self-sufficient."

"Like a doomsday bunker?" I had not seen anything suggesting that, or I am sure I would have remembered.

"If you want to call it that," he explained. "I told Wendy that she can design it however she wants from the ground up, as long as I get to design the underneath. So down there we've got living space, power, heat, communications, food, water, and all sorts of supplies. I even stocked up on everything that could become currency when the monetary system fails. Things like ammunition, alcohol, cigarettes, and even insulin. When the apocalypse comes, that's where we're heading."

"The zombie apocalypse, right?" I was joking, but I was also intensely curious. I had been researching how the uberwealthy were buying or building shelters for their families to ride out a major catastrophe.

"More like the collapse of the global ecosystem after the US self-destructs," he replied, growing quite serious. "Just like what happened after the fall of the Roman Empire. We've been seeing signs of the decline for years, so it's just a matter of time before all hell breaks loose. We're just one crisis away from catastrophe. A military conflict gone haywire, a global pandemic, a prolonged economic downturn, an over-contentious presidential election, a natural disaster. You name it. This country is being held together by toothpicks and duct tape right now, so just about anything could be the spark that sends us over the edge and potentially into a civil war. In fact, historically speaking, we're probably overdue for a major shakeup."

I was bursting with excitement that I was finally getting to speak with someone who believed the same as I did. My research had led me down this path, so I knew this was a growing concern. I just had no one in my inner circle who shared it with me. "I'm so glad you think this! I've been telling Julie the same thing for a while now, and she thinks I'm just being paranoid. It's nice to find someone else who thinks the same."

"Well, here's a scary story," Stockton replied. "I've got friends who work on Wall Street. They tell me that every day they go into the office prepared for a major sell-off. Their firms have strategies and protocols in place to avoid another disaster like last year's. Essentially, if they get even an inkling that there will be a market downturn, they're under instructions to dump as many of their holdings as possible to cut their potential losses."

"But that would collapse the economy!"

"Exactly what I told them. They agreed, but it's a matter of self-preservation. Like I said, we're just one crisis away from the apocalypse."

So far, I was following Stockton's logic, since it mirrored mine. There was just one strategic detail that stood out for me. "Why Canada?"

"First, it's close to Seattle, so we can make sure we get there okay, even if the airlines shut down. Second, it's remote, so we can avoid all of the looters, marauders, and other mayhem that will happen. And I'm trying to get Canadian residency and eventually a Canadian passport. When the shit hits the fan and the US collapses, I want to be a Canadian citizen living in Chile."

We arrived back at the hangar parking lot, and Stockton dropped me off at my car so we could both head home. Over the years, he and I would have many long talks like this, especially during flights, boat rides, and sub dives. I would come to value his insights as well as the opportunities to share my own.

A month later, I was in our new home sharing with Julie about the last part of my talk with Stockton in the car. I admitted to her that I felt completely unprepared to protect our family. Stockton not only had his place in Canada, but he also had vital survival skills. As an engineer, he could build or fix just about anything. He had even learned how to farm and dig water wells. Also, he could operate just about any vehicle on land, sea, or air. I had none of those skills. I felt like I was letting down our family. When the apocalypse came, we would be screwed.

Our daughter, Rebecca, was only ten years old, but she was sitting nearby and overheard us. She tried to cheer me up by saying, "Don't worry, Daddy. If it comes to that, we can just go stay with Stockton."

The next day, I told him what she had said, and he laughed. "Yeah, you can get in line behind all of my other friends who think the same thing!"

October 2009

Boulder, Colorado

"Why'd you pull over?" Julie asked from the passenger seat of our minivan.

We were on the interstate just north of Boulder, where we had spent a few days visiting my sister and her family as part of our cross-country relocation trek. Our three kids were in the back seat. It was snowing lightly as we made our way through the Rocky Mountains, heading toward our new lives in Seattle.

I had just hung up from a conference call with Stockton, Graham, and his wife. It had not gone well.

"The deal just fell apart," I said.

Even though we had all come to a verbal agreement that weekend in Canada, we still had to formalize the legal documents for each of us. Stockton's capital investment and my employment contract were executed in just a few days, but Graham's intellectual property assignment and employment contract had become way more complicated. Despite Stockton's best efforts to give Graham everything he wanted, they were just too far disconnected on some final points in the company structure. During that fateful conference call, they mutually agreed to terminate DeepFlight Technologies and go their separate ways.

Of course, this impacted me and my family the most, since we were already two-thirds of the way across the country. We had already sold our house in Virginia, shipped all of our household goods, transported my car to Seattle, and pulled the kids out of school. This was not an ideal turn of events for us.

"So what should we do?" Julie asked.

Fortunately, Stockton had anticipated that something like this might happen and fully appreciated the significant risk Julie and I were taking. He was incredibly generous in helping us get through this.

"Well," I said. I thought carefully about my next words. "We could keep going straight to Seattle. Stockton has already offered to keep his word about funding the company and paying me to be its CEO, even if we lost Graham. Then again, I just met the guy a couple of months ago and now we have no technology or CTO. Or we can turn left and go to San Francisco. I'm sure I could continue working with Graham, as I have for the past year. Of course, he really can't afford to pay me. Or we can turn around and head back to Virginia, and we'll figure out another plan."

She replied immediately. "Well, turning around is not an option, since we have no house there, and all of our stuff is on its way to Seattle. And since we need a paycheck, it seems like the answer is clear, right?"

Of course, she was right. I put the car in gear, and we continued our trek across the Rockies.

October 2009

Everett, Washington

THE BLANK WHITEBOARD STARED OUT AT US, AND WE JUST STARED BACK. Stockton and I sat in the small, nondescript conference room in our hangar, alternately looking across the table at each other and up at the whiteboard on the wall. We needed to figure out a business plan for our new venture.

Without Graham, DeepFlight Technologies really had no business. We had no intellectual property, and we had no CTO to create any. All we had was me, Stockton, and our commitment to each other. Well, that and a desire to use crewed submersibles to help humanity improve life on Earth.

We tackled this problem using a method that I still use to this day and have passed on to many other entrepreneurs.

On the left side of the whiteboard, we listed every asset he and I had at our disposal, including his seed capital, my time, each of our experiences, our professional networks, our respective skills and educational backgrounds, and so on. On the right side, we listed every problem or obstacle facing humanity when it came to the oceans, whether in exploration, science, education, or conservation. Then we drew lines between each side, connecting assets on the left to the problems on the right that they could address. We ended up with a mesh network of crossed lines. Finally, we evaluated each line and ultimately picked the one that resonated the most with both of us.

The problem that bothered Stockton the most was the severe lack of sub availability for anyone who wanted to dive to any significant depth. During that planning session, he went on a rant that I heard him repeat many times over the years and that I have also made myself.

"There are only a few dozen subs in the world, which is ridiculous given how huge the ocean is and how little we know about it," Stockton pointed out. "And none of them are available for charter. I should know, because I tried to charter one! Most of these are relatively shallow subs sitting on the decks of billionaires' yachts for joyrides. If you want to dive deep, like beyond 2,000 meters, then your only choices are six subs owned by five national governments. And that's not even reaching the average depth of the ocean, which is about 4,000 meters, let alone the deepest point at 11,000 meters. Humanity deserves better."

"If you're a researcher in Ecuador and want to use a sub to study the ecosystem around the Galapagos, you're pretty much screwed," he continued. "Your only choices are (a) wait a few years for one of the government subs to make their way to the Galapagos and hope you can get a seat on a dive, or (b) convince the Ecuadorian government to spend millions on building their own sub and millions more per year to operate it. Imagine if you could just charter a sub for a two-week expedition for a few hundred thousand dollars!"

While I completely agreed with his assessment and shared his conviction on the value that a sub charter business could provide to humanity, my passions lay along a different path.

"Maybe I've got too much Silicon Valley in me," I started. "Or maybe I've been working for too long with space entrepreneurs. Whatever it is, I'm convinced that humanity will someday live and work in underwater cities. And not in some far-off sci-fi future, but within the next fifteen or twenty years. We already have some underwater habitats used for science, and there are even some underwater restaurants and hotels. If we really wanted to do something disruptive, maybe we could create the first deep-sea fully pressurized habitat? Something like an ISS for the oceans, a place where a dozen scientists could spend significant time studying the ocean environment."

There is a long-established rule for brainstorming sessions: There is no such thing as a bad idea. I was pushing the envelope, and to his credit Stockton let me fully articulate my thoughts. Then he brought me back to reality.

"Look, I'm 100 percent with you on the habitat idea," he chimed in after I had finished my rant. "In fact, that'd probably be a great place to go when the apocalypse hits. The only issue is that any business along those lines will be so capital-intensive that my seed funding is not going to get us very far. I think we have to find a focus that's more within our financial reach. I think we're going to need to stick with subs for now."

"Yeah, I know you're right." I could feel my body sagging from the disappointment.

"Well, look at it this way," he said, trying to cheer me up. "When those underwater cities are ready, people will need a way to travel to them and back, as well as between them. They're going to need subs. So let's create a business that provides them."

It worked. I felt better. Unfortunately, we still needed to figure out a new business model for our sub startup.

"Okay, it sounds like a charter business might be the way to go, right?" I looped us back to his original idea.

Actually, once we got to that point in the brainstorming session, the rest flowed quite quickly and effortlessly. This was due to our being able to lean into our shared passion for space.

"We both know that the oceans suffer from the same problem as space." Stockton tried to summarize our discussion. "Namely, lack of access. And we both know that the lack of access is caused by the high cost of access. Elon saw this and created SpaceX specifically to drive down the cost of access to space by at least one order of magnitude, if not more. We need to do the same for the oceans. We need to be SpaceX for the oceans."

We both liked the sound of that tagline, but we also knew that we could never say that publicly. The scale of effort would be comparing apples and oranges. Neither of us would ever presume to be on the same level as Elon or SpaceX. Of course, we could certainly use it as an internal motivational motto for us and our future team.

"I like that," I said. It was time for me to pick up the thread. "So what makes SpaceX so special? We both know that their first innovation was not technology but business. They disrupted the industry by charging NASA for a ride to space rather than selling them rockets. Instead of building and selling cars, they started a taxi or trucking business. Of course, they would've been screwed if some folks at NASA hadn't been visionary enough to follow suit and change their own way of doing business, but hey, it's worked out for everyone so far."

"Right, so maybe that's what we need to do," Stockton said, continuing my line of reasoning. "After all, we don't have a CTO or technological IP. Can we create enough of a disruptive cost-reduction simply by changing the business model? Can we lower the cost of access to the deep oceans by an order of magnitude simply by chartering subs rather than selling subs? If so, then all we have to do is buy an existing sub and make it available for charter."

"Well, as you keep pointing out, it's the difference between buying a sub for millions or chartering one for a few hundred thousand," I offered. "That sounds like enough of a disruption to me."

"I agree," he said. "Then again, SpaceX also has technology innovation. They're focused on using reusable rockets to drive down launch costs even more. Aren't we also going to need some new sub technology to really make a difference in access to the deep oceans?"

"Maybe," I replied. "But if we can reduce costs by an order of magnitude just by offering a charter model, then that's a great start. If someday in the future we find that we also need some technology innovation, then we can look to buy something, to contract something, or to hire a new CTO to design and build something. In the meantime, sub charters are probably enough."

"Okay, but it can't be just one sub," he said. "Again, SpaceX doesn't have just one rocket to provide the rides. Even though our sub will be reusable, we will probably need more than one, right? I mean, the cost of transporting a sub anywhere in the world could get ridiculously expensive. What if we had four or five of them pre-positioned around the world? That would help drive the costs down even more without needing any new technology innovation."

"That's a great idea," I said. "But remember that you killed my underwater habitat idea because it was capital-intensive. You're not going to put up the money to buy five subs, are you?"

"No way," he replied. "But I'm sure we can find investors to finance the idea, especially since those will essentially be asset-backed investments. Let's start with one sub and build up from there."

We fell silent and looked at each other. We looked at the whiteboard. We looked back at each other. Then we laughed.

We had figured out our new venture's founding vision: *to own and operate a small fleet of deep-diving submersibles that could be deployed anywhere in the world on a charter basis.* And Stockton would pursue this vision with every fiber of his being from that day in the conference room until the day he perished near the bottom of the Atlantic Ocean.

"If we can pull this off, we'll open the oceans for humanity to better understand our planet," he said. "We can provide a gateway for people to go into the ocean. Remember the movie *Stargate*? Well, this will be like 'OceanGate.'"

A few days later, we renamed DeepFlight Technologies as OceanGate, and we purchased the domain www.opentheoceans.com.

November 2009

Everett, Washington

We struggled with the first few steps. We both knew the famous saying about journeys of a thousand miles beginning with a single step, and yet we were stuck on the second or third. We had two co-founders, some seed capital, a founding vision, a name, and a URL. And an airplane hangar for an office. Now what?

If only it were as simple as purchasing the subs for our fleet and beginning operations as a charterer. We could certainly try that route, but we already knew that it would require much more capital than Stockton was willing to invest himself. We would have to raise money from outside investors, which fortunately we both had experience doing and were willing to do. For that effort, we would need to hone our new business model, starting with finding the right subs for our new fleet.

Before raising the money to go sub shopping, we needed to know exactly what kind of sub we wanted to buy. Specifically, we needed to come up with a list of basic requirements that would fulfill our business needs.

Keeping in mind that our objective was to drastically reduce the cost of access to the deep oceans, we had to do everything we could to keep our own costs as low as possible. This drove the first few requirements:

- **Purchase price of $5 million or less:** We ran a number of calculations, and no matter how much we changed the assumptions, this seemed to be the natural ceiling for how much could be spent on the sub itself. Anything higher than this would force us either to charge more for the charters and forgo our target cost reductions for end-users, or to take way too long to recoup any investor's principal.

- **Light enough to require no more than a ten-ton crane:** Submersibles require a surface support ship to launch and retrieve them at a dive site, so the ship has to be fitted with a large enough crane to handle the weight of the sub safely. The size of the ship dictates the maximum size of the crane, with bigger ships able to hold bigger cranes. Unfortunately, larger ships burn through more fuel, and fuel is *by far* the most expensive cost in sub dive operations. The heavier the sub, the larger the crane; the bigger the ship, the higher the fuel cost. Therefore, the best way to keep operational costs down is to use the lightest subs possible.
- **Small enough to fit inside a standard 40-foot shipping container:** Even though we had visions of a fleet of five subs pre-positioned around the world, we would still have to ship those subs within the region to wherever our customers needed them. The best way to reduce transportation costs would be to use standard shipping containers that could be sent anywhere in the world.

Beyond those three cost-driven requirements, we also came up with two mission-related requirements. This exercise actually forced me and Stockton to think clearly about why we were so drawn to sending humans underwater versus, say, tethered remotely piloted robots or autonomous preprogrammed drones.

Our rationale was based on our shared passion for exploration, which we believed had the power to inspire and educate people in ways that very few human activities could. If NASA had taught us anything, it was that people are inspired by other people much more profoundly than they are by machines. After all, the Apollo astronauts became heroes and role models in ways that none of the Mars rovers could ever achieve.

Our shared desire to help humans go places underwater where no one had ever gone before in order to explore and inspire others shaped our next two requirements:

- **Carrying capacity of five people:** Most deep-diving subs carried one to three people, including the pilot. There were many reasons for this, but regardless, we did not believe three-person crews would be sufficient for our purposes. After all, this would mean that the maximum crew would be a pilot, a scientist, and a storyteller. We wanted the ability to also carry a second scientist, since the underwater environment required many different scientific disciplines, such as oceanography, marine biology, and nautical archaeology. Also, we thought that the storytellers might be better as a team, such as a camera operator and an on-air host or narrator.
- **Expanded physical visibility:** The industry standard design for deep-diving subs was a titanium spherical hull with small circular acrylic or glass viewports, often no bigger than a person's face. The only way to see anything underwater was to lie on your stomach and put your face against the window. However, some of the shallower-diving recreational subs were made of acrylic spheres, so

they offered a 360-degree view of the ocean environment, making dives a literally immersive experience. We wanted something closer to that than to the small portholes.

Our final requirement was based on our mission to expand humanity's knowledge of our ocean planet, acknowledging how vast those oceans have always been:

- **Depth rating of at least 4,000 meters (ideally, 6,000 meters):** By many estimates, humans have explored less than 5 percent of the world's oceans, mostly because they cover more than 70 percent of our extremely large planet. The average depth of the ocean is estimated to be approximately 4,000 meters. A sub rated to this depth would give us access to about 65 percent of the world's oceans. Then again, 6,000 meters would increase that footprint to 98 percent. Only 2 percent of the world's oceans lie between this and 11,000 meters, primarily in just a few very deep but narrow underwater chasms. If we really wanted to help humanity explore the oceans, our target had to be 6,000 meters, but we would settle for 4,000 meters, if needed. Of course, there would be a financial trade-off, since the cost of building a vessel that could withstand the immense pressure at those depths rose almost exponentially the further down the sub had to travel safely.

Armed with those six basic business requirements, we set about researching what sub builders could potentially meet our needs.

Back then, as now, the global submersible community was tiny. If we wanted to buy new subs, then we had only a few choices of vendors:

- **DeepFlight:** This was Graham's original company, and the one we had hoped to merge into our newly created but failed DeepFlight Technologies. As difficult as it would be on a personal level given the failed startup partnership, we could consider hiring Graham to build us a fleet of his winged submersibles.
- **Triton Submarines:** Arguably the gold standard for crewed submersibles, this Florida-based company was run by Patrick Lahey, a former commercial diver who became one of the most experienced sub pilots in the world. They built some of the safest and most beautiful subs, catering to the most demanding clientele: wealthy individuals with exquisite tastes and a penchant for adventure. Although they also built some commercial tourist subs and ensured their subs could handle science and film missions, their sweet spot was putting their high-end machines on expensive yachts.
- **SEAmagine:** Co-founded by brothers Charles and Will Kohnen, California-based SEAmagine built subs for work and recreation. Will, an aerospace engineer by education and profession, became an ambassador for the global sub community, leading the only sub-focused membership group, conducting annual conferences, spearheading standards and regulations, and collaborating with classification organizations and government agencies.

- **U-Boat Worx:** This Netherlands-based company built a few lines of subs that extended from two to seven passengers, for recreation and commercial uses. They created a niche for themselves providing subs for cruise ships to offer as additional activities for their passengers. This was a visionary long-term strategy because it involved collaborating with the cruise ship builders early in the ship design process.
- **Nuytco Research:** Founded by Phil Nuytten, one of the godfathers of crewed submersibles, this Canada-based company had pioneered some of the early sub designs, ranging from single-person atmospheric diving suits to large multi-passenger tourist subs. It was Phil who had given Graham his first job in the sub world many years prior. He was well-respected and even revered by everyone in the community.

There were other one-off sub builders, but generally that was it. Five small sub builders, each producing one or two subs per year. That was the entirety of the global sub "industry" when we started OceanGate. Sadly, this is still true today.

Stockton and I were already aware of these five vendors, and we already knew there would be issues with each of them.

All of them shared the common business model of selling subs to buyers who would then own and operate them, much like Ford, Ferrari, or Honda. On the other hand, we were taking a completely different business approach, and we needed to buy a bunch of Fords in order to operate our taxi business.

We knew upfront that their current designs would not meet our business requirements, at least not all of them.

This would have to be a collaborative long-term strategic partnership, and we knew it would be an uphill battle. However, if we could find at least one of them willing to give it a shot, then we believed that we could raise $30 million to cover the cost of building a fleet of five subs and the eighteen- to twenty-four-month runway to get us through the build process. Our first opportunity would come in February, when the community was scheduled to get together in New Orleans for its annual conference.

In the meantime, we had to consider alternatives.

These partnerships would all offer new subs, but there were plenty of used subs scattered around the world. We began an extensive search, hoping to find one of them coming on the market soon, even if it did not meet all of our requirements. We were anxious to start operations quickly, and a used sub could fulfill that objective.

Very early in our search, we found Pete Hoffmann in Florida.

For several years, he had operated a business that designed, built, and sold various marine vessels. In the late 1990s, he had purchased a twenty-year-old decommissioned diver lockout sub called PC-1501. Built by UK-based Perry Submarines, these subs were the workhorses of early underwater commercial operations, and this one in particular had three compartments. The aft end contained a diesel engine for propulsion, the middle section was a hyperbaric chamber that acted as a lockout system for saturated commercial divers, and the forward section was for the two pilots. Since that forward section was its own pressure vessel, Pete separated it and transformed it into a small crewed submersible capable of taking five people down to 305 meters.

He managed to sell it to a wealthy Russian businessman for his yacht, but a couple of years later he was asked to resell it. He found a New Zealand–based commercial buyer, who wanted to use the sub for a tourism operation.

Once the sub arrived on-site, it was rechristened *Antipodes*, in homage to a British term for New Zealand. The word "antipode" refers to any point on a sphere that is diametrically opposite another point, such that a straight line connecting the two would pass through the center of the sphere. On a globe, the North and South Poles are considered antipodal points. Likewise, New Zealand and Great Britain.

The commercial owner used the sub for a few years before filing for bankruptcy, so once again Pete was asked to resell the sub. That is precisely when Stockton and I came across his online posting.

We discussed this opportunity and ultimately decided it could be a critical strategic first step for us into the world of submersible operations. The sub did not come anywhere close to meeting our depth requirements, but it certainly fulfilled the others. Even though we would be limited to shallow-diving missions very close to shore, we thought it would be the perfect way for us to take our first baby steps as a new venture. If we could strike a deal with the bankruptcy trustee through Pete, then we could potentially become the new owners of a sub that was old but proven and trusted.

Pete was asking $295,000 for the sub and replacement parts, which was within the budget parameters of the seed capital Stockton had committed to fund OceanGate. Stockton made him an offer for the full amount, sight unseen. He had already spoken with Pete and liked him immediately. He did not want to get into a lengthy negotiation with him and certainly did not want to lose the sub to another prospective buyer. I flew out to Florida for a final inspection, and then Pete put the sub on a flatbed trailer and had it shipped to Seattle.

We decided to keep the name *Antipodes*, but for our own reasons. While it made historical sense for the sub's prior Kiwi owners to use that name, we needed the name to mean something special for OceanGate. After a little research, we discovered that only 15 percent of the world's land masses have antipodal points that are also on land. The rest are on water. That's how immense this planet's oceans are. No matter where you live, the odds are that the point directly across from you on the globe is an ocean. It is your antipode.

OceanGate had a sub, and we would be ready to roll into 2010 as the newest entrants into the small community of submersible operators. We were on our way!

December 2009

Pompano Beach, Florida

PETE AND I SAT INSIDE THE SUB. IT WAS A BIT SURREAL BEING IN *ANTIPODES* while it was parked inside his garage at the end of a suburban cul-de-sac, but it made for a nice "conference room."

Pete was a soft-spoken, kindhearted, worldly man with cropped white hair and a full beard to match. He had spent the bulk of his seventy years on the ocean, so he looked every part the seasoned, salty mariner. He exhibited a boyish enthusiasm for subs, but he and I clicked mostly due to our common bond as former US Marines. I had flown to Florida to conduct the final inspection before he shipped the sub to Seattle, and he was immeasurably patient with me as he gently and calmly walked me through the intricacies of my first submersible purchase.

We had already checked the outside and inside of the sub, and he had told me the story of how he originally built it. We had even gone through all of the logs and documentation. The guys with the crane and flatbed truck were not scheduled to arrive until the next morning, so we had some time to kill before having lunch and spending the rest of the afternoon packing everything for the cross-country drive to Seattle.

Pete had decades of industry experience, and I could not pass up the opportunity to tap into that vast reservoir of knowledge. I wanted to use our downtime sitting in the sub to pick his brain on some questions that had been plaguing me.

Because Stockton and I wanted our initial foray into the sub world to be as flawless as possible, we wanted to make sure that we complied with every single regulation, especially those related to safety. He reiterated many times that he was counting on me to use my legal background to keep us compliant, but for me it was like drinking from a firehose. The regulatory regime was a labyrinth, starting with the very basic concept known as "classification," or "classing." Generally, this was a process by which sub builders got a third-party organization to review their work. That part was clear to me. After that, it all got fuzzy.

"So, Pete, can you explain this whole classing thing to me?" I asked. "Since Graham Hawkes designated all of his subs as 'experimental,' I've never had to deal with the classing process. Stockton and I want to make sure we keep *Antipodes* classed, so what do I need to know?"

"Geez, where to start?" he said. "Well, you know about the American Bureau of Shipping, or ABS, and Lloyd's Register, right? Those are the two main classification groups that work with manned submersibles right now."

"Yeah, the two classing agencies."

"Well, they're not really agencies, since they're not part of any government. They're basically private enterprises."

"They're not government agencies?" I suppose I should not have been surprised that such a tiny global community would be operating without any regulatory oversight. "You mean, they're not charged with protecting the public's safety?"

"Nope."

"So they're not funded by taxpayer dollars?"

"Not as far as I know. I believe they generate revenues by selling their services."

"And they stay in business by classing subs? That sounds like a horrible business model."

"No, no," said Pete, laughing slightly at my naivety. "Their primary business is classing ships, especially commercial ships." Ah, that made more sense.

"So what do they do with subs?" I was still reeling from the fact that the two classing groups were not government agencies and that they did not really focus on subs.

"They basically develop safety standards for the design and operation of subs, and then we all have to prove to them that our subs comply with those standards. If we can do that successfully, then they give us a certificate."

"So the certificate says that the sub is safe?"

"Hell no! Are you crazy?" he scoffed. "Can you imagine the legal exposure for ABS if they signed a certificate that says *any* vessel was safe?"

I felt stupid. With all of my legal training, I should have seen that coming. "Well, then what does the certificate say?" I asked sheepishly.

"It just says that the sub complies with current standards."

"That's it?"

"That's it."

There had to be more to it. From the very beginning of our journey into the sub world, all Stockton and I ever heard about was how important it was for subs to be classed.

"Well, what does the certificate get us?" I probed.

"Honestly, not much. Sometimes an insurance company may require that you have one. Sometimes a regulatory body may require that you present one before operating in their jurisdiction. That's basically it."

"Well, then why do Triton, SEAmagine, Nuytco, and U-Boat Worx make such a big deal out of it?" I was truly confused.

"Ah, because they are in the business of selling subs to owner-operators, and the certificate is a huge selling point for those customers. Which makes sense, right? I mean, if you were going to buy a complex vehicle that you had to trust with your life and the lives of your passengers, then you'd definitely want some proof from a third-party group of engineers that it had been built properly, wouldn't you? I mean, you wouldn't just take the builder's word for it."

"Yeah, that makes total sense, but Graham told me it can cost a lot of money and take a bunch of time."

"For a sub like *Antipodes*, no, not really. She was ABS-classed as PC-1501, and she's still classed today. You just have to go through the renewal process. She's a typical old sub that I built in compliance with long-established standards for manned submersibles. Even after I chopped off the pilot section from PC-1501, ABS was actually quite reasonable because I tried as hard as possible to keep everything else as compliant as possible."

"Wow, that's not how Graham explained the process to me!"

"Of course not," said Pete, "because that's not the process that Graham has had to deal with. He's not in the business of building subs that comply with existing standards. He's in the business of developing completely new sub designs for which there are absolutely no preexisting standards. Even if he submitted a certificate application to ABS or Lloyd's, they wouldn't know what to do with one of Graham's flying sub designs."

"So that's how Triton and the rest of the builders get through the classing process? They make sure that their subs comply with currently accepted engineering and operations standards?"

"For the most part. I mean, they're always coming up with new innovations here and there, but as long as they generally keep to the standards that ABS and Lloyd's are used to, they're usually okay."

"Well, that makes sense, too. After all, in order for those guys to maximize profits, they need to keep their costs as low as possible. One way to do that is to mass-produce their subs, or at least to sell product lines with some standard features and a limited number of customizations. I could see that. Too bad they don't sell that many units per year, because they're amazing machines. It'd be nice if there was more market demand for their subs."

"I'm sure they'd agree!"

"Okay. This is all great, but now you've got my mind spinning with a million more questions!"

"That's fine. We've got plenty of time. Ask whatever you want." Pete was such a patient man.

"Well, let's get back to *Antipodes*. It's already classed by ABS, but that certificate is expired since the bankruptcy took so long. What's the process for us getting everything current and then keeping it current going forward?"

"A bit cumbersome, but manageable. I can put you in touch with the right person at ABS, and then he'll walk you through everything. The main thing you'll have to do is take the sub through what's called a 'special survey,' which is a rigorous inspection process that you'll need to do every three years. Basically, you have to take the sub apart completely, like, down to the hull. Then you have to schedule an ABS inspector to inspect everything. Then you have to put the sub back together, and bring the inspector out again for another inspection. Then you need to take the inspector on a dive to the full rated depth of the sub, which in our case is 1,000 feet."

"So the inspector has to come out three times?" I asked.

"Yup."

"And we have to completely disassemble the sub and put it back together?"

"Yup."

"And during that time we can't dive the sub?"

"Obviously."

"And how long will this process take?"

"That depends on how well organized you can be and how proficient your team is. And of course the inspector's availability. It could take a few weeks or maybe even as long as six months."

"What?"

"But I think most likely it can be done in two months."

"Still, ouch!"

"At least you have to do that only every three years, so it's not that bad," Pete said. "In between, you'll have to conduct two annual surveys, but those are not nearly as detailed and don't require the disassembly or the dive."

"I guess doing that every three years is not that bad," I admitted. "Besides, it's probably a good practice to do this as part of our safety protocols anyway."

"Oh, I almost forgot. They'll also need to review your dive logs and operations manuals. You can probably use the ones from New Zealand, but obviously you'll have to customize them to your particular needs. This may take you some time, but then again, you'll only have to do this once."

"Ugh! You're going to be available to help walk us through this, right?"

"Of course. Stockton and I already discussed this. No problem."

We climbed out of the sub and took a break for lunch at a local diner. My head was still spinning with all of the classing stuff. Stockton had made it clear that he wanted me to be in charge of this part of the business, since it would probably benefit from my legal background and would require my level of attention to detail. This loomed as a critical element of our competitive differentiation, so I was feeling the growing pressure on me to get it right every step of the way.

The list of questions was expanding exponentially in my head, so after we placed our food order I jumped right back in. "I think I'm starting to wrap my head around all of the ABS stuff related to *Antipodes*, so maybe we can shift gears to what comes after this for us?"

"Sure. What do you want to know?"

"Oh, wait. I had one last question on *Antipodes*. You said that Triton and the other builders need their subs to be classed because it's a selling point with their customers. Stockton and I have already decided to keep *Antipodes* classed, but do you think that we *have* to do it? I mean, we're not planning to sell this sub or any others to customers. We're just going to operate our subs and charge people for the service. Do you think customers looking to charter our subs will require that we have classed subs? Do you think any of them will ask to see *Antipodes*' ABS certificate?"

"I'd have to ask the previous owners, but I'm pretty sure that no one ever asked them for that certificate in the entire time they dove the sub in New Zealand. Hell, I seriously doubt anyone outside the sub community even knows what that is!"

"Oh, so we don't even need to maintain *Antipodes*' class certificate if we don't want to?"

"Well, hold on," said Pete. "You asked me if any of your charter customers would ever ask for the certificate. My answer is 'most likely, no.' However, like I said before, there may be others who could require it. Again, I'd have to ask the prior owners, but I wouldn't be surprised if the New Zealand government asked them for some sort of certificate. Even if they didn't, they probably required them to carry some sort of insurance, and the insurance company may have asked them for a third-party certificate. Most agencies don't know anything about subs, but they tend to know boats, so they'll ask for the same paperwork they would ask from a boat operation. And this usually includes an ABS or Lloyd's certificate."

"Oh, right. I get it. Unlike the sub builders, our customers may not ask for the certificate. However, just like the sub builders' customers, we may be asked for it by other outside agencies or organizations."

"I think I followed that, so yes, that sounds right."

"Got it."

"You wanted to talk about what comes after *Antipodes*?" By then, he was already picking at his salad. I was impressed by his mental acuity, given that he was as old as my dad but much quicker with his analytics and more solid with his memory. I had already lost track of my own thoughts, but he still remembered where I had intended to take the conversation. Sharp mind.

"Yes, thanks. So you already know that our long-term vision is to have a fleet of deep-diving subs. Essentially we need five *Antipodes*, but lighter, smaller, and capable of diving to 6,000 meters."

"And I already told you that none of the builders currently have anything like that available. They'd have to custom-build them for you."

"Exactly. That's where I have more ABS questions."

"Alright. Go ahead."

"You mentioned that the process for *Antipodes* and for almost all of the sub builders' current subs is fairly manageable in large part because those sub designs typically comply with generally accepted sub standards that ABS and Lloyd's are familiar with."

"Yup."

"But the subs we're going to need will have to be different designs. In fact, they may have to be radically different designs," I said. "I'm guessing that whoever we partner with to build these subs will not be able to do it within their current lines of subs."

"I can 100 percent guarantee you that they will have to come up with new designs."

"So what will happen when we take those new designs to ABS for them to give us a certificate? What if our designs don't comply with any accepted standards because they're too new and innovative? What if there are no standards for our designs because we're breaking new ground and blazing new trails? After all, you can't have 'standards' for something that's being done for the first time."

"Well, this is the problem that Graham had with trying to class his flying sub designs, right?"

"Yes! Exactly."

"Honestly, I'm not sure what that process would look like. But I do know it would take time and money."

"Oh, crap! Right. I forgot to ask about costs."

"It depends on each sub. For *Antipodes*, the special survey probably won't be much more than a few thousand dollars. However, to get a new sub design certified, I have no idea. I wouldn't be surprised if it was hundreds of thousands of dollars. And it'll take quite a bit of time, depending on how radical the new designs are. For something like Graham's flying subs that are also made of carbon fiber, I wouldn't be surprised if it took a couple of years or more to get them classed."

"Shit!"

"And it's not just the calendar time. It's also your team's time. Or the time of whoever you partner with. After all, they're going to have to walk the ABS engineering team through all of their designs and most likely have to educate them on the innovations. Like with Graham, he'd have to spend months teaching ABS about winged subs and carbon fiber."

"But that would be ridiculous," I said. "He's the world's leading expert on winged subs and probably one of the leading experts on carbon fiber. How could he possibly transfer that much knowledge to some ABS engineer? It doesn't even matter if that engineer is the best engineer in the history of humanity; he still wouldn't have the hands-on experience that Graham has built up over the course of his career."

"Yeah, well, that's how new standards get developed. Not just for subs, but for any industry."

"Maybe. But manned submersibles is not an 'industry.' We're too tiny for that. There aren't enough of us out there to churn out that many new designs or experienced engineers."

"I guess now you can appreciate better why Graham never seemed to get along with the classing agencies. And why he referred to his subs as 'experimental' vessels, since those don't need to be classed."

"So let me make sure I've got this straight," I said slowly as I gathered my thoughts. "Let's say we partnered with Triton to build us five subs to meet our business requirements. And let's say we wanted them to be classed by ABS. If Triton can build the subs we need with only minor modifications to one of their existing designs, then classing them will be fairly straightforward.

However, if they have to come up with a radical new design—like adding wings or using carbon fiber hulls—then classing them will be a nightmare that could cost us hundreds of thousands of dollars and take up months, if not years."

"You got it."

"And all of this just on the off chance that some jurisdiction or insurance company ever asks us for the certificate?"

"Yup. It's a risk-reward analysis you and Stockton will have to make."

"This sucks! And I'm assuming that Lloyd's will be the same, right?"

"Yup."

"And those are our only two options?"

"Yup."

"This sucks!" I exclaimed again.

"Yup."

"Why would anyone ever voluntarily go through this process?" I was completely flabbergasted. I had dealt with standards before in other industries, but this was just bonkers. I had never seen a process that was so ridiculously broken.

"Well, there are other benefits to getting a certificate from ABS for a new sub design," Pete offered. I got the feeling that he was starting down a line of reasoning that he did not quite buy into. "After all, in your hypothetical, we just talked about how the process would require Triton's engineering team to walk the ABS engineering team through every aspect of the design. This effectively provides a pretty good sanity check on Triton's engineering team and on the design itself. Like a third-party engineering peer review."

"I could see that, but there are so many other ways to get the same type of peer review. In fact, there are probably better, more effective, and more efficient ways."

"How?" He stopped eating, put down his fork, and folded his hands in front of him. He seemed genuinely curious about how someone could get around this.

"Well, ABS cannot possibly have a monopoly on the best sub engineers in the world. I can't see Triton or Nuytco ever conceding that point. I'm sure the ABS engineers are great, but they can't possibly be the best in the world. And, almost by definition, they can't be the only ones in the world."

"Obviously, you're right about that."

"In fact, I'll take it one step further. I could argue that relying on the ABS team to provide the engineering peer review on a new sub design could be considered negligence on the part of the sub designer."

"What? How?" He wanted very much to agree with me, but I could sense that I might have gone a step too far with that last assertion.

"It's the cop-out easy way to check the engineering peer review box. 'Rather than finding the most talented and experienced subject-matter expert in the world, we'll just go to ABS and get them to look at our stuff.' What the heck kind of commitment to safety is that?"

"I think I see where you're going with this," he said slowly, as he pondered my train of thought. I felt like I was making progress, and I was getting myself excited with the arguments forming in my mind.

"Here's a not-so-hypothetical example," I said. "Let's say that we partner with Triton to build our fleet of five subs, and they come up with an innovative new design based on a carbon fiber hull. Stockton and I would be completely negligent if we relied on the ABS engineering team to conduct the engineering peer review on Triton's design work, because no one at ABS knows anything about carbon fiber hulls. Instead, we should insist on hiring, say, Graham Hawkes to do the peer review. The proper way to approach a robust engineering peer review is to go after the most capable engineering team for your design. Simply relying on the ABS team because they can also provide us with a class certificate just seems ridiculously negligent. I would never use that as a justification for going through ABS."

"I never looked at it from that angle, but I see your point." He smiled and picked up his fork to continue eating.

I felt like I was finally starting to understand the whole process, so I leaped ahead to some natural consequences of my perspective. "Wait. This doesn't even make sense from a safety standpoint, either."

"Why not?" I could tell that he was still mulling over my last point, so he was only partially ready to listen to another one.

"If we have Triton come up with a new innovative design, then it will be the first of its kind. If we can get ABS to accept it and give us a certificate, then it will become a new industry standard that ABS can use to assess similar designs submitted by us or any other builder in the world."

"Correct." That part was easy. Next came the hard part.

"But how does ABS even know that this new design Triton created for us is safe? I mean, it'll be the first of its kind, so until we've been operating it for a few years, no one will really know if it's safe. What if there's an inherent flaw that we all missed during the design and testing process? What if it only emerges after, say, five years of operations? And what if in the meantime ABS had classed multiple other subs based on the same 'standard'?"

"Yeah, that'd be a problem." I was making it difficult for Pete to enjoy his lunch, but it looked like he was following my logic.

"Even worse, what if the design Triton came up with was not the best way to achieve our ultimate objectives? What if there are better ways to do it, and we come up with them later but then it's tough to get those approved by ABS because they don't meet our own original designs that they're now using as 'standards'?"

"You lost me. What do you mean?" I knew I had pushed too far.

"Well, let's look at a different example. We know that right now James Cameron is racing to get the solo sub dive record to Challenger Deep. His team is developing a new design to reach the deepest part of the ocean, and it's completely different from the one Graham previously developed for Steve Fossett, before he died a couple of years ago. Obviously, none of them were trying to get an ABS class certificate, but what if they had? As of right now, the only design that ABS could use as any sort of reference would be the *Trieste*, which the Navy dove in 1960. Would that be the standard, even if it was the only one of its kind? If so, then neither of the two modern designs would comply. They would both have to get their designs certified by ABS, in which case they would then have three different industry standards, which is an oxymoron. New builders would not know which one to comply with. And again, none of them would have a proven safety record."

"I think I followed that. Yeah, it sounds right."

"That's ridiculous! How many different airplane designs did the Wright brothers go through before they succeeded at Kitty Hawk? How many did they go through afterward? I don't understand how a first-time design can ever be accepted as an industry standard, since that's not what it is by definition. And even if you can get a first-time design to be designated as an industry standard, then that just throws the whole 'classed equals safe' argument out the window."

"Welcome to the world of safety standards," Pete said simply.

January 2010

Everett, Washington

STOCKTON AND I SAT AT THE SMALL CONFERENCE TABLE. FROM THE INTErior rooftop "office" overlooking the hangar floor, we could keep an eye on *Antipodes*, our new "training wheels sub," as we went on to call it. We were in high-powered planning mode, the only gear that Stockton had.

We knew that we would need some time with *Antipodes*. We had to get the sub diving again after it had spent extended time sitting in a shipping container waiting for the prior owner's bankruptcy proceedings to run their course. It had originally been certified by ABS, so we would need to get back its classed status. Finally, we would have to get trained on how to pilot and operate the sub. We estimated that all of this would take several months.

In the meantime, we were scheduled to attend the sub conference in New Orleans the following month. That is where we would finally get to speak with each of the various sub vendors and try to negotiate a partnership for a fleet of new subs. After all, *Antipodes* was a workhorse sub, but it was old, heavy, and cumbersome. We were not sure if it would adequately serve our business model. Regardless, it was just one sub, and we needed four more.

Whether we ended up having to round up a few more used subs or got lucky and found a partner for a fleet of new subs, we knew that we were going to have to raise significantly more capital. Stockton said that he could potentially put in some more of his own money, but not nearly enough to cover everything we were going to need. That afternoon, we got together to plot our fundraising strategy, and it took an interesting turn.

"Hey, here's a strategic question for you," I said after we'd been speaking for an hour or so. "Do you think we're more likely to get traction with equity investors or with philanthropic donors?"

"You think we should become a nonprofit?" Stockton asked. I was always surprised by how quickly his mind worked. He had already jumped ahead in my thought process, so I struggled to catch up. He was a nonlinear thinker, and he relied on me as a linear thinker to always take a moment to assess if he had skipped over anything critical. Our rapid-fire exchanges often led to almost comical interactions where one of us would get frustrated with the way the other's mind was working.

"I'm just brainstorming. After all, we have a social mission to 'open the oceans.' You and I are driven more by exploration than anything else. And we're doing this to help humanity. Right?"

"Interesting," he said, already understanding where I was going with this. "I guess we never really made a conscious decision to create OceanGate as a for-profit venture. It just seemed like a natural continuation of DeepFlight Technologies. But that had a completely different mission and business model that lent itself only to a for-profit approach. Hmmm . . . it could work."

"If we wanted, maybe we could create a sister organization, like the OceanGate Foundation," I suggested. "Then we could start fundraising and see whether we get more interest from investors or from donors. If it's investors, then we give them equity in the for-profit company and keep the nonprofit as a supporting organization. If it's donors, then we give them a tax deduction and hire the for-profit company as a vendor. Heck, we could even go all-in and merge the for-profit company into the nonprofit. That would streamline everything."

"Let's do it! Why don't you start working with the lawyers to get that going?" Stockton thought fast, talked fast, and acted fast.

"Okay, I'll get on it." Man, that was quick.

However, I had been meaning to ask him some questions that were more personal than business. "Shifting gears," I prefaced, "How're you holding up? I feel like you're already spending way more time on this than you originally wanted."

"I'm definitely spending too much time on this."

"When we started, you said no more than eight to ten hours a month. I'm guessing you're doing at least that much *per week*."

"At least. It's not good. I'm starting to move around some of my other board commitments, but I'm still CEO of that other small company. I have to figure out how to rearrange my life so I can do more of this. Especially once we start diving *Antipodes*."

"And how's Quincy doing?" His daughter was dealing with some personal issues that weighed heavily on Stockton. Every family copes with some level of problems, and his was no different. Wealthy or not, people are people, family is family, and parenthood is parenthood.

"She has her good days and bad days. It's a struggle, especially for Wendy. At this point, it's a whole family effort. They need me there, and I want to be there for them. It's just difficult spinning so many plates. Besides, those two women are way stronger than I am, so I'm not even sure where I'm adding value."

"Well, I'm sure they appreciate your making an effort for them."

"I guess so."

I could tell that he was not entirely comfortable talking about this, so I switched topics back to OceanGate. "Speaking of rearranging your life, are you sure you want to come to New Orleans? It's going to be a lot of talking, networking, and schmoozing. Not exactly your favorite activities."

"No, I'm looking forward to it."

"It's just that when we started, you told me that you wanted me to be the CEO so that I could be the public face of the company. You said that you're a private person and don't want anyone to know you're involved."

"I still don't like the public part, but I'm curious to meet all of these guys."

"Hopefully we'll find someone who wants to work with us," I

said. I was apprehensive that we would come back without a partner and have to reassess our entire business plan.

"And hopefully they'll fit our 'no assholes' policy," Stockton retorted. He was much more concerned about making sure that we dealt with people we respected and trusted.

"Of course, that's one of my favorite policies. Life's too short to work with people you don't enjoy being with. Fingers crossed we can keep that going."

"Agreed."

Chapter 5

INTO THE FRAY

June 2023

Barcelona, Spain

I BARELY SLEPT ON WEDNESDAY NIGHT. THAT THURSDAY MORNING, I GOT up at 4 AM, which was 1 AM in the middle of the Atlantic and 7 PM Wednesday night in Seattle. Still no news from the search and rescue teams. If the crew was still alive and trapped in the sub, then they had only hours left in their emergency life support. Time was running out quickly.

I scanned all of the media outlets, and the negative stories about Stockton continued to pour out. It was a relentless barrage. The company was still silent, and no one seemed to be coming to its defense.

Meanwhile, my phones, emails, and social media were still overflowing with interview requests from journalists around the world.

At some point during my sleep-deprived night, a part of my brain snapped, and I decided that Stockton's voice in my head was right: I had to speak up.

It went against every professional instinct I had, against every piece of advice I had received, and against every self-preservation fiber of my being, but I knew that I could not live with myself if I passed up the opportunity to do something and say something.

One way or another, I was certain that the news cycle would shift within twenty-four hours. By midday on Thursday, the search and rescue teams would either have to find and save the crew or change to a recovery operation after the sub's life support reserves were exhausted. Even if I was right and the sub had imploded on Sunday, it could take days before the wreckage was discovered. Regardless, by then the news cycle would have shifted away from *Titan*.

It was now or never.

If I was going to have any chance at all of fighting the negative narrative against Stockton, then I was going to have to move quickly. I needed a global platform to push against the global media phenomenon, so I might not get another chance. Once the news cycle shifted, there would be no chance to regain the kind of widespread attention I would need.

I could not believe that I was actually considering this, even after three days of suffering. I tried justifying what I was about to do by telling myself that my "co-founder" title tied me to OceanGate forever, so I had to say something in order to protect my own professional reputation and my own current projects. I also rationalized that I had no exposure to legal liability since I had left the company before we began to develop *Titan* and I had never been on one of our *Titanic* expeditions. I even caught myself saying out loud in my apartment that the field of ocean exploration deserved a better defense, so that it could continue to benefit from the kind of innovation OceanGate was built for. And the list of excuses went on and on. Anything to make me feel better about potentially destroying my life on a public stage.

Then I thought about Stockton.

Assuming he was still alive and about to be rescued, he would probably be fine with everyone's decision to remain silent. As an intensely private person, he had never been a big fan of the media, so he would understand no one wanting to subject themselves to a public lashing. However, if the roles were reversed and it was me in the sub, then I knew for certain that Stockton would have taken the first opportunity to jump in front of cameras to push back against any inaccuracies or negative commentary. He would not have waited for three days, like I had. Then again, he was more impulsive than I was. Or maybe I was more deliberate than he was.

In any case, I prepared myself for what was about to happen.

I did not have a PR team to help me, so I was going to have to rely on my prior media training as a CEO and board member. I tried to remember everything I had been taught about crisis management. I was able to get a hold of a friend who is a PR professional, and he gave me some last-minute coaching.

First, I had to temper my expectations and remember how the modern media industry worked. Producers, journalists, editors, and publishers were there to do their jobs, not to cater to my wishes. I had to help them get ears and eyeballs, clicks and likes, attraction and engagement. I had to play my role in their game. In exchange, they might allow me to get a few points across on their platforms.

Second, I had been trained to focus on no more than three primary messages. Always answer the interviewer's question directly first, and then weave in at least one of my messages. I thought carefully about what my three messages were going to be, and I wrote them down as succinctly as possible: (a) the Stockton I knew was not the Stockton being portrayed in the media; (b) Stockton and the rest of the OceanGate team and the *Titan* crew were driven to help humanity explore the world's oceans; and (c) it would be weeks or months before we had enough evidence to determine what went wrong, so we should all avoid speculating. I practiced them aloud until I felt comfortable that I could get them out even under the pressure of a quick-fire interview.

Finally, I created a spreadsheet with all of the media outlets that had reached out to request an interview. I prioritized them based on global audience size. Then it would simply be a matter of reaching out and scheduling the interviews.

I knew that once I popped my head up, it would be a madhouse. My girlfriend was not a PR person and in fact was quite private, but she wanted desperately to support me. The best she felt she could do was to keep track of the interviews for me, which, as it turned out, would be a massive undertaking.

I decided that the first three interviews would be BBC, Fox News, and CNN, so I crafted my email and text replies to each of their inquiries. I told my girlfriend, "This is going to be either the worst thing that ever happened to me or the best."

I took a deep breath and pressed "send."

The responses came quickly, and the interviews were scheduled immediately. Before I knew it, I was on a video call with each of the three journalists. As those segments went live, my inboxes started lighting up with even more requests from even more outlets. Since this was exactly what I was hoping for, I agreed to every request that came in, and before I knew it I was booked for back-to-back interviews nonstop for hours. My girlfriend was frantically trying to keep the spreadsheet updated so I would not double-book myself in any time slot. Also, while I was conducting interviews, she was watching or reading the previous interviews in order to help me hone the messaging going forward. It was a crazy day, but at least I finally felt like I was doing something useful.

Then, in the middle of the chaos, everything changed.

The US Coast Guard held a press conference to announce that they had found *Titan*'s wreckage and to confirm that all five members of the crew had perished in an apparent implosion on Sunday.

It was a sickening blow, knowing that Stockton was dead.

But it was softened somewhat by the fact that I had suspected an implosion from the beginning—I had been preparing myself for this news the entire week. Also, the news did not change any of my three primary messages, so I could continue with the interviews that had already been scheduled.

The one significant change after that press conference was my sense of urgency. With the implosion and deaths confirmed, I knew that I had only a few hours left before the news cycle would shift to some other major story. There would be plenty of time later to deal with the consequences of my decision to take this course of action, but in the heat of the moment, I had to stay focused. I had to push hard to complete as many interviews as possible before the spigot shut off.

I was right, because by Saturday morning media outlets around the world had dropped the OceanGate tragedy from their headlines and front pages. As quickly as it began, the media frenzy was over. The deaths of the five *Titan* crew members, including my friend Stockton Rush, were suddenly old news.

In all, I finished twenty-one interviews in less than forty-eight hours. Some were with major outlets, like Anderson Cooper at CNN. Some were with local outlets, like a radio station in my birthplace of Buenos Aires, Argentina. *The Wall Street Journal* sent a camera guy to my Airbnb in Barcelona. An entire production team was deployed by *60 Minutes Australia* to interview me at a local hotel and marina. It had been exhausting, but Stockton's voice inside my head had kept me pushing on. As difficult as this had been for me, I knew in my heart that I had done the right thing.

After I finished the last scheduled interview on Saturday, I collapsed. I had not had time to process everything that had just transpired, including the fact that Stockton was gone. I knew it would take some time for that reality to sink in.

Likewise, I knew it would take some time for me to grasp what I had just done to my life by throwing myself into fray.

As it turned out, the effect was quite immediate.

Chapter 6

INNOVATION IN OCEAN EXPLORATION

February 2010

New Orleans, Louisiana

WE STOOD TOGETHER AT OUR GATE AT THE LOUIS ARMSTRONG INTERNATIONAL Airport in New Orleans, waiting to board our flight back home to Seattle.

"So, what'd you think?" I asked. We had not yet had a chance to debrief after our first time attending the Underwater Intervention annual gathering of the world's submersible designers, builders, and operators.

"Honestly, I wasn't that impressed," Stockton replied, almost exactly as I had anticipated. After all, he had high standards, and it took a lot to impress him.

"Why not?" I asked.

"Well, first of all, we already knew that the global sub community was small, but geez, we had everyone who is anyone in that small room for three days."

"Agreed. To call it an 'industry' is so misleading."

"And I just got the impression that the same guys have been getting together for years talking about the same things and building the same subs in the same way without any real innovation."

"Yeah, it kinda made you appreciate Graham's flying subs, right? Even though they attacked him at the time, at least he was thinking outside the box," I said. As a nonengineer, I was still in awe of Graham's novel idea to use inverted wings on subs to overcome buoyancy to dive underwater the same way an airplane uses its wings to create lift to fly in the air.

"Well, that's the thing. Almost all of them are in the business of selling subs to wealthy buyers, so they just find a nice safe product that works and just keep pushing it out," he said. That "product" was basically an ABS-classed two- or three-person shallow-diving sub with a spherical acrylic pressure hull capable of operating off a yacht and diving 300–600 meters, available for $2 million to $5 million in eighteen to twenty-four months.

"You can't blame them for that," I said. "In fact, that's exactly what we were originally hoping to do with DeepFlight, wasn't it?"

"Yeah, that's true."

"Then again, that's not our business model now."

"No, that's definitely not our business model now. It doesn't help push humanity forward. That barely gets just a few of us exploring our coastlines. You know how damn big the ocean is. We need to take more people deeper and on a more regular basis. We need to live our motto, and 'open the oceans.'"

"So what do you think this means for us going forward?" I asked. I had already been mulling over this question during our various conversations with everyone at the conference those past few days. "I mean, we have *Antipodes*, but we already know that's not our future. We can't have a global fleet of ancient heavy shallow-diving subs."

"I don't know. I got the sense that none of these guys could help us. Or want to help us."

"Well, they're certainly willing to sell us one or more of their subs," I said. It had been abundantly clear even to me that all of the builders at the conference saw Stockton simply as a rich guy with lots of money to spend on a sub.

"Which would've been perfectly fine, if any of their subs actually met our requirements," he said.

"Or if they were willing to build us new models that did."

The biggest pushback we heard from our various conversations was that we could not get everything we wanted in the same sub. The shallower subs could meet most of our requirements, except, of course, depth. Getting a sub to the deep ocean, especially down to 4,000 meters and beyond, would require a hull strong enough to withstand extreme pressure.

On dry land—and on the ocean's surface—we experience the weight of all the air directly above us in the atmosphere, which is roughly 14.7 pounds per square inch. For shorthand, we also call that "1 atmosphere" or "1 ATM" of air pressure. When we start diving underwater, we also feel the weight of all the water directly above us in the water column. Since water is much heavier than air, the pressure increases much more rapidly. Specifically, it adds 1 ATM every 10 meters, which means that the pressure is 2 ATM at a depth of 10 meters, and so on. By the time we reach a depth of 4,000 meters, a sub experiences pressure that is four hundred times greater than on the surface. In order to withstand such extreme pressure, subs have traditionally been constructed out of titanium hulls that are quite thick and therefore very expensive and heavy.

"I just refuse to believe that, with twenty-first-century technology, no one can build a lightweight sub that can carry five people and dive to 6,000 meters for less than $5 million," Stockton said. He was getting riled up. "I mean, c'mon! This is probably how Elon felt when he tried buying a rocket for Mars and couldn't find one that fit his requirements."

I feared he would bring us back to the SpaceX analogy that we had already used when we founded OceanGate. "So does this mean what I think it means?" I treaded lightly.

"We're going to have to do the same thing Elon did with SpaceX," he confirmed. "We're going to have to build our own subs."

And there it was. The huge strategic shift that would drive OceanGate for the next decade.

"Well, how the hell are we going to do that?" I asked the obvious question. "We don't have a CTO, remember? And we're set up as a sub operator, not a sub builder. Not to mention that we're still trying to figure out how subs even work, which is why we got *Antipodes* in the first place. Do you think that maybe we can hire any of these guys on a contract basis to help us with a new design?"

"Who?" he asked skeptically.

"I don't know. I was pretty impressed with Don Walsh and Phil Nuytten," I said, going through my mental Rolodex from the past few days.

"Yeah, those guys were impressive," Stockton conceded. "We should definitely follow up with them. At least they seemed to appreciate what we're trying to do for ocean exploration."

"How about Will Kohnen or Patrick Lahey?" I asked, as I continued down the list. "I know they'd prefer that we buy one of their subs, but maybe they'd help us on a contract basis? I mean, Will's certainly an experienced engineer, and Patrick's one of the most prolific sub pilots in the world."

"Maybe, but I don't know if they'll be able to get out of their own heads to fully embrace what we'll need." Stockton was back to being skeptical. "I feel like they'd be fighting us the whole way. We're going to need some out-of-the-box thinkers. Mavericks."

"Like Graham?" I asked. This was a rhetorical question, since I knew he was not an option after the failed partnership on DeepFlight Technologies. "How about that Karl guy? You two seemed to hit it off pretty well."

"Karl Stanley? Yeah, I really liked him," he said, cracking a smile. "He's a little crazy with the way he built his sub in Oklahoma and operates it unclassed in Honduras, but he certainly doesn't like conventional thinking. Maybe. We should keep in touch with him, too."

"Wait a sec," I said. A worrisome thought suddenly occurred to me. "You keep saying 'we,' but do you mean me? Am I going to follow up with all of these people? I'm not sure I'd know what to say to them or how to engage them on designing and building a new sub. I mean, I've dealt with technical teams on technical projects before in other startups, but I've always had my technical co-founder in those conversations."

"No, I'll do it," he said.

"You will?" I was not buying it.

"Yeah, why not?"

"Um, because you don't have time for this, remember?" I said. "You've got your other companies. You want to focus on your family. You can only give us eight to ten hours per month. Doesn't any of this sound familiar?"

"Yeah, yeah, yeah. I'll figure out something," he said. Then he turned serious. "We have to get this done. It's why we started this company, right?" He grew quiet, and I could tell his mind was going into rapid-fire mode.

It was getting busy around the gate as our flight began to board, so we had to table the rest of our conversation. I felt like we had made a huge decision that would greatly impact the future of our young startup.

For better or worse, we were about to transition into the world of deep-diving submersible design and manufacturing. And neither of our lives would ever be the same.

March 2010

Everett, Washington

STOCKTON AND I WALKED SLOWLY AROUND THE SUB. *ANTIPODES* WAS parked in our hangar, but neither of us could believe that we actually owned a real sub. Only a few months after losing Graham and starting OceanGate from a blank whiteboard, we had our first sub!

It was a far cry from the fleet of deep-diving subs that we imagined in our founding vision for the company, but we had to start somewhere.

We were anxious to start diving, so for the past month I had been researching the regulatory framework for diving subs in US waters. Graham had already spooked us with his stories of run-ins with the Coast Guard, and my limited research confirmed why he had had so many issues.

Stockton had made it clear from the beginning that he wanted me to use my legal background to take the lead on this part of the business. As much as he typically chafed at rules and regulations, he was keenly aware that we needed to stay on the Coast Guard's good side in order to avoid getting shut down. That was a business risk neither of us was willing to take, so he insisted that we fully comply with every single regulation out there.

"Do you want to talk about my research into the Coast Guard regs?" I asked.

"No, but I guess we have to," he replied. "At least let's go sit inside the sub for this conversation."

Once we were comfortably in the sub, I sat in the forward dome while he sat in the pilot's seat and constantly fidgeted with every switch, knob, dial, valve, and cable.

"Ready?" I asked.

"Sure. Whaddya got?"

"Well, let's start at the beginning. Right now, there are only three manned submersibles operating legally in US waters with Coast Guard approval. All of them are shallow-diving tourist subs owned and operated by Atlantis Submarines out of Vancouver."

"How'd they get past the Jones Act restrictions?" he asked.

"You're getting ahead of me!" Sometimes his fast mind could be frustrating. "But the short answer is, I'm not sure. As you obviously already know, according to the Jones Act, all vessels operating in US waters have to be designed, built, and operated by US citizens or companies. I have no idea how a Canadian company got past this. Maybe they have a US subsidiary? Maybe the individual owners are US citizens? I don't know, but I'm sure they figured out something legal, because they've been operating with the Coast Guard's blessing for over twenty years."

"What about all of the Triton and SEAmagine subs?" Stockton began probing. "Those guys are based in the US. Don't they have any subs diving in US waters?"

"Nope. All of their customers operate their subs either overseas or in international waters," I replied. I immediately recognized a gap in my response, so I had to move fast to close it before he jumped on it. "Well, let me rephrase that—all of their *commercial* customers. I imagine that some of their wealthy American customers who put the subs on their yachts for personal use might occasionally dive them in US waters with their friends and family. I can't say for sure. We'd have to ask them."

"And what about the research subs?"

"Well, obviously *Alvin* is a government sub and operates under its own rules, and you already know that most of the other private research subs have been decommissioned. If you mean the two or three subs that occasionally get research contracts from NOAA and other research agencies to do some dives in US waters, then as near as I can figure, they're operating without Coast Guard approval. When I spoke with them, one was under the impression that they didn't need Coast Guard approval to do dives with NOAA scientists and another one told me that they've been doing dives for years without the Coast Guard saying anything."

"So they just get a research contract, head out to the dive site with the paying scientists on board, and just hope that the Coast Guard doesn't notice and shut them down in the middle of a dive?" Stockton was incredulous.

"Sounds like it," I confirmed.

"That's idiotic. We can't do that. All it takes is one Coastie having a bad day to decide that enforcing the law might be a good idea, and they'll completely ruin our entire business."

"At least in US waters."

"Right. So how do we do it legally? Can we just do exactly what the Atlantis guys are doing?"

"Get ready to have your head spin," I said, preparing him for what was coming. "I'm not sure if I can even explain it coherently, so I'll just start and you jump in when I'm not making sense."

"As always."

"First, you can imagine that the regulations are a nightmare. There are almost no subs operating in US waters. We don't know which caused which, but either way it's going to be bad. If there are no subs because the regs are bad, then that's bad for us now since we'd have to figure out how to comply with crappy regs. If the regs are bad because there are no subs, then that's bad for us in the long term since we'd have to convince the Coast Guard and potentially even Congress to fix the regs just for us. Either way, we're screwed. Just to set your expectations here."

"So far, no surprises. Go on."

"Okay. As far as I can tell, there's really only one relevant regulation for subs, and it's not even a full reg since it's just a guidance memo issued in 1993. Also, there seems to be only one person in the Coast Guard who has any sort of expertise on subs, and he's sitting at HQ in DC. Fortunately, he's extremely helpful and supportive, at least as far as his job duties will let him. Also, Will Kohnen has been a great resource, since it's in his committee's best interest to make sure that us OceanGate newbies come out of the starting blocks in compliance with all the rules."

"Actually, now I'm surprised," Stockton said. "I didn't think the Coast Guard would have even a single person who knew anything about subs, let alone someone at HQ. I mean, why would they? There are only three operating subs way out in Hawaii, Saipan, and Guam, and they've been doing it for years. Really only the local Coasties in those sectors need to know anything at all about subs."

"Interesting. I hadn't looked at it that way, but you're right," I said, always thankful for his unique perspectives. "Anyway, this guidance memo is called—hold on, I have it here on my phone—the *Navigation and Vessel Inspection Circular No. 5-93*, shortened to NAVIC 5-93. The actual title is *Guidance for Certification of Passenger Carrying Submersibles*. And, yes, they use 'certificate' as a verb, not just a noun, which was new to me."

"Geez, you take forever to get to the point," he complained. "You and your linear thinking! Just spill it. What's the bottom line? Are we going to be able to operate in US waters or not?"

"Okay, okay. I'm still getting used to your nonlinear thinking!" I said. "The bottom line is that we *may* be able to operate in US waters, but we're going to have to squint really hard and try to shoehorn ourselves into some cracks between the regs and then hope that we can find some friendly sector commanders.

Otherwise, we'll have to do what everyone else does and operate outside US waters."

"I was afraid you'd say that. I'm probably going to regret asking this, but how do you propose we do this? You're the lawyer, so do some of that lawyer shit." We were both *Top Gun* fans.

"Well, first I'll tell you what will *not* work. We won't be able to do what Graham does and designate our subs as 'experimental' vessels, because then we can't take paying customers. I think Graham gets away with his 'sub pilot schools' because it's a small operation and he tries staying away from active Coast Guard sectors. We also can't be a 'personal' or 'recreational' sub, like your old Kittredge, for the same reason."

"Geez, I didn't ask what we *can't* do, I asked what we *can* do. Get on with it!"

"This leaves only two general categories: tourist subs and research subs. Each is allowed to carry paying passengers."

"But as a charterer, we won't have any control over what our customers want to do with our subs," he said. His mind was already racing ahead of me. "What if a yacht owner wants to charter *Antipodes* for his family vacation? If we are the operator, is that considered a tourist operation or a personal or recreational operation? What about a filmmaker who wants to shoot a documentary from one of our subs? That doesn't seem to fall under any of these categories."

"Like I tried telling you, we're going to have to shoehorn ourselves into some of the cracks between the regs. It's entirely possible that we may have to limit our US operations to only a few use cases for certain specific customers. For everyone else, like filmmakers, we may have to dive somewhere else."

"Well, it sounds like the tourist category is the most generic, so why can't we use that one?"

"Honestly, because it's the most limiting. It sounds like that particular category was written specifically with the Atlantis subs in mind, so to comply with it, we'd have to operate like them. They basically do shallow laps around a small lagoon in huge subs carrying forty or fifty people. The Coast Guard treats them just like they would a ferry boat. They have to operate along a predetermined path on a predetermined schedule. Also, get this, the sub pilot is required to have a valid hundred-ton captain's license."

"What? That's ridiculous!"

"I thought you'd like that. I also thought it was crazy. At first. But that's mostly because you and I are both looking at this through our *Antipodes* lens. Why would our pilots need a hundred-ton license for a seven-ton five-person sub? But you've seen those Atlantis subs. They're freakin' massive! I could totally see why the Coast Guard would want the Atlantis sub pilots comfortable operating large ships."

"I guess," he conceded. "Anyway, we can't operate on a preset anything. Every one of our charter customers is going to want to dive somewhere different and follow different dive plans. How would we ever comply with these requirements?"

"We can't. Not with our business model."

"Dammit! Will you just skip ahead to your point already?" Sometimes I found perverse pleasure in getting him riled up by forcing him to follow my linear thinking.

"Sorry. This leaves only one possible category: research. As near as I can figure, the Coast Guard wanted to let American scientists continue using subs, so they simply took the existing rules for oceanographic research vessels that they use for surface ships and modified them for subs. These regs give sub operators much greater flexibility when it comes to the sub's design and build requirements, safety standards, operational parameters, and crew qualifications. I believe that *Antipodes* would easily qualify as an ORV. Then all we would have to do before we dive anywhere is to connect with the local sector commander and submit our mission plan. It sounds fairly straightforward."

"I feel a 'but' coming."

"Actually, several 'buts,'" I said. "The first one is obvious. This only works for research missions. In fact, one of the primary requirements that we have to include in the mission plan for the sector commanders is the science objective for every dive."

"So no filmmaking, personal use, oil and gas, military, or anything else? We would have to limit our customer base to only scientists? That's not nearly a big enough market for our business model."

"Right. Well, remember I said we might have to squint a little," I said. "On this point, it might be enough to simply make sure that every dive has a science objective. Theoretically, we could charter the sub to a filmmaker and just assign a science objective to every one of their dives, even if it's not relevant to their film's plot."

"Sneaky, but legal. I like it!"

"Don't get too excited. I haven't mentioned the worst part yet."

"Dammit! You're killing me! What's the bigger issue?"

"Well, our entire objective is to carry paying passengers. But as an ORV, we'll be limited to carrying only three categories of people in the sub: owners of the sub, members of the sub crew, and members of the research team. No one else will be allowed on board."

"So how do we get filmmakers or anyone else on board?"

"That's the part you and I need to discuss, because I think we'll need to work through several options."

"Such as? C'mon, this is like pulling teeth!"

"Well, let's walk through each one. The first is owners. If someone paid us to charter a sub, we could theoretically give them a small equity stake in our company. Say, a fraction of a share? Then technically they could be considered 'owners' of the sub."

"Again, sneaky but legal. I like it."

"Do you? Really?"

Stockton thought for a second and reconsidered his initial response. "Nah. It'll be a pain in the ass. Can you imagine how many shareholders we'll end up with after a few years of operations? The admin costs alone would kill us. Let's keep going."

"The second category is members of the crew. Again, if someone chartered one of our subs, we could theoretically hire them as temporary crew members. Maybe we give them a limited contract and pay them a dollar just for nominal consideration? Filmmakers would be easy, I think, since they could be considered part of our production crew. For others, we might have to give them some training beforehand."

"It's not ideal, but for some folks that might actually be a selling point. They could train as our comms person or something. I don't know about giving them a contract because that sounds like another admin headache."

"Hey, I tried warning you that none of these will be ideal solutions."

"I know. Weren't there three categories? What about the last one?"

"Researchers," I said. "We could theoretically assign each of our charter customers to be in charge of a specific set of science objectives for each dive. I don't think we'll need to have an actual scientist on each dive, but it would be good to have someone to somehow supervise the science portion of our dives and have the paying passenger act as the field research assistant to help collect data, even if it's just photos, sonar images, or log entries."

"That could work. Instead of being part of our ops crew, they'd be part of the science crew. It'd probably be cleaner that way. And more defensible with the Coast Guard."

"That's what I thought. This might be our best path forward."

"So why didn't you just lead with that?" Stockton asked, exasperated.

"C'mon, Stockton, you know our brains work differently. It hurts my head to jump around the way you do. Just as much as it hurts your head to try staying focused while I trudge slowly along a straight line from start to finish."

"Yeah, yeah, yeah. Whatever," he said mockingly. "So that's the solution, right? We designate *Antipodes* as an ORV, we hire a science director to make sure every dive has a science objective, and we assign every paying passenger as a member of the science team. Then we file the proper paperwork with each sector commander, and we're good. That doesn't sound too bad. It's messed up, but not too bad."

"One last thing."

"Crap! You're driving me crazy!"

"Well, this is a practical implementation issue rather than a regulatory one," I explained. "The Coast Guard recognizes that every sector is different, and so they give each commander a fair amount of leeway to exercise discretion in applying regulations within their sector. This means that even if we get approved to operate as an ORV in one sector, it does not necessarily guarantee that it'll work in another one. We're going to have to go one by one and hope that we find open-minded commanders wherever our customers want to go."

"So getting approved here in Seattle doesn't get us a free pass anywhere else?"

"Correct. And there are something like thirty-plus sectors. It'll be hit-or-miss, so we'll have to work closely with each of our charter customers and set proper expectations that our plans may be declined."

"What a pain in the ass! I can see why everyone else either avoids the US or risks asking for forgiveness rather than permission."

"Exactly. Hopefully this approach will work."

"Well, there's only one way to find out. You might as well start with the Seattle sector. If we can't operate here in our home sector, then we're screwed anyway."

"I already started pulling together the paperwork," I replied. "Fingers crossed!"

April 2010

Puget Sound, Washington

I LOOKED UP AND SAW THE SKI BOAT'S PROPELLER ZIP OVER US ONLY twenty feet from *Antipodes*' acrylic dome. Instinctively, I ducked my head, not so much because of that particular boat but more because I knew there were other boats speeding our way and the sub was still ascending. I figured we were likely seconds away from a massive collision, and I shot a quick worried glance to Stockton, who was perched in the other dome at the opposite end of the sub.

Just a few feet from the surface, the pilot, Tym Catterson, was finally able to stop our ascent, and the sub began to descend quietly back into the darkness of Puget Sound. I watched with quiet relief as the ceiling of boat propellers faded out of sight. He held us level at 100 feet, just so we could all catch our breath and assess the situation.

After identifying the cause of the problem and determining that we could resume our ascent safely, we called up to the support vessel once again for clearance to surface. On the other end of the radio was Ursula Ginster, who confirmed that the boat traffic had cleared. We climbed back to the surface, and the rest of the mission went as smoothly and safely as we had originally planned.

During the ride back to the marina, I replayed the entire incident in my mind. Specifically, I tried to learn from Tym and Ursula, the two-person team we had hired to come teach us how to dive *Antipodes*. They had been the Chief Sub Pilot and the Operations Director, respectively, for the tourism operator in New Zealand that had previously owned *Antipodes*. They had logged over four hundred safe dives in our sub, so we figured they would be the perfect instructors for us.

When we returned to shore, we held an all-hands debrief. We reviewed every aspect of the mission, but obviously we spent considerable time discussing the near-catastrophic initial ascent. The team determined two critical contributing factors.

First, the "uncontrolled ascent" we experienced was caused by a stuck release valve that prevented Tym from venting one of the ballast tanks on the way up from the bottom of our dive. As the sub ascended and the water pressure dropped, the air bubbles inside the tanks grew bigger and created more lifting force, which in turn increased the rate of the sub's ascent, perpetuating the cycle. On *Antipodes*, the release valves were the primary mechanism for controlling the size of those air bubbles and therefore the ascent rate of the sub. If the pilot did not—or could not—maintain a vent rate equal to the rate at which the bubbles were growing inside the tanks, then the pilot would lose control of the sub and could not stop it from surfacing.

Normally, this would not be a huge problem. After all, before lifting off from the bottom of Puget Sound, we had called to the surface and requested clearance to come up. They had checked the surroundings and determined there were no obstacles for us on the surface, so they had given us the green light. Even with an uncontrolled ascent, we should have been fine.

However, there was a second contributing factor.

We were diving in a part of Puget Sound that was not too far from the Ballard Locks. This is a series of two locks that connect Lake Washington to Puget Sound, and they are large enough to carry several small boats across the canal. In the spring, dozens of locals take their boats out of winter storage in Lake Washington and bring them out onto Puget Sound for a rare day of fun in the sun. When the locks open and release the boats, it can seem like the start of a sprint race, with a flurry of boats suddenly spilling out and speeding off in different directions.

Unfortunately for us on that day, Ursula was not familiar with this phenomenon in Puget Sound and was not properly briefed by anyone on our team. She was an experienced sub operations chief, but she had never dived in Puget Sound. When we initially called up for permission to surface, she looked around and saw no boat traffic, so she gave us the go-ahead. However, after we started our ascent, the lock opened and suddenly there were boats all over the area where we were likely to surface. She immediately called down for us to halt our ascent, but that is when Tym realized that he had lost control of the sub and could not stop us.

As usually happens with accidents, the cause is typically a confluence of several rare events that combine to create tragic situations. None of them is catastrophic on its own, but together they can spell disaster.

We survived that day mostly due to Tym's quick thinking based on his years of experience, but that led to an honest conversation between me and Stockton after everyone had gone home.

"Is there anything we could've done differently?" I asked. "I mean, since we started this company, we've tried doing everything by the book, and yet we still almost died today. What else could we have done?"

"Nothing," Stockton said. "Every expert we've talked with told us to do things this way. The ocean is an unforgiving place, so sometimes shit happens, even if you do everything exactly the way everyone thinks you should do things."

In retrospect, that incident was probably the first time Stockton and I both started viewing the current submersible community with skepticism.

He and I were outsiders, coming to the ocean world via our shared childhood passion for space exploration. Recognizing that we did not know what we did not know and that we had way too many blind spots, we started our OceanGate journey in the most conservative manner possible:

- We purchased a used sub that had already conducted over seven hundred successful dives for two previous owners.
- We made sure that the sub was classed by ABS, since at the time that was the gold standard for classing societies.
- We took the sub through a special survey, which was the comprehensive inspection required for all classed subs conducted every three years.
- We hired *Antipodes*' designer and builder, Pete Hoffmann, as a consultant to help us through the entire classing process and to provide initial pilot training for me and Stockton.
- We hired Tym and Ursula to train us on how to properly conduct dive operations. Not only did they have direct experience with *Antipodes*, but Tym in particular was—and continues to be—one of the most experienced and respected sub pilots in the world.
- We even did something that most sub operators did not bother to do (for a variety of reasons): Namely, we developed a relationship with the local US Coast Guard sector, so that they would be aware of our operations in Puget Sound.

Even in those early days of OceanGate, Stockton and I started to see the opportunity—and need—for continuous innovation and market disruption. Just because everyone did things a certain way or just because that was how things had always been done did not necessarily mean that it was the best way or even the safest way.

That day in Puget Sound, we did things exactly the way every expert told us to do them, and we still almost suffered a major catastrophe. Maybe—just maybe—those "experts" did not have all of the answers after all.

May 2010

Puget Sound, Washington

WE HAD TO START DIVING. FAST. IF WE WERE GOING TO BECOME THE world's leading charterer of deep-diving crewed submersibles, we had to hone our skills as sub operators. We did not necessarily need to have the best subs, but we certainly needed to have the best ops team. This meant everything across the entirety of an expedition, including expedition leaders, transportation logisticians, mission directors, science directors, surface support ship coordinators, shore base commanders, crew managers, communications officers, boat drivers, and, of course, sub pilots and technicians.

We believed that the only way to get good at something was to just do it, so that was exactly what we set out to do.

As soon as *Antipodes* was ready to dive, we got started with an incremental training program designed to hone our skills one step at a time. Initially, we did shallow dives on a wreck in the protected waters just outside our marina in Everett. Then we went out into deeper water in the middle of Puget Sound, sometimes just for exploration but often with a specific target or scientific objective. Our team was coming together nicely, so we started training with non-OceanGate "guests," like scientists, educators, and filmmakers. We were still far from being ready to open for business as a charterer, so these were all still practice exercises.

Along the way, we developed processes and protocols for everything from mission planning and pre-briefs to launching and retrieving the sub with the marina's crane to towing the sub behind our support boat to crew transfers using an inflatable dinghy to dive operations and communications to post-mission debriefs to emergency response and crisis management. We also had to coordinate our operations with the US Coast Guard to qualify as an ORV, so we filed dive plans with our sector command before our missions and communicated with the watch command before we left the marina and after we returned.

Stockton and I would continually assess our progress and plan next steps. We would grow and train the team to match our objectives. It seemed that every day we were learning more and more, usually from things we did right but often from mistakes we made. After a while, I noticed that most of our protocols were derived to avoid repeating mistakes, which I found often was the best way to learn anything.

For example, a couple of our safety procedures were derived from a single incident at the end of a dive just outside our marina in Everett.

The dive plans for *Antipodes* during near-shore dives included having the support boat tow the sub out to the dive site and back. This was accomplished by securing a tow line from the stern of the boat to the tow bridle hooked onto the braces at one end of the sub. Someone would stand on the deck of the sub, catch the tow-line tossed to them by the boat's deckhand, and tie a proper knot with the line through the noose in the bridle. In calm waters, that person would stay on the deck of the sub during the tow, so that they could be ready to release the line when we arrived at the dive site or at the marina.

The person on the sub's deck was typically a trained sub pilot, but they did not really have to be, since all they were doing was tying and untying a knot. It could be anyone, as long as they knew the proper knot to use. Or so we thought.

After a training dive on a local shipwreck, one of our deck-hands asked if she could "ride the sub" back to the marina. As the acting Mission Director, I approved, so she secured the tow line and perched herself on the sub's conning tower for a leisurely ride home.

As we were slowly working our way through the entrance to the marina, we heard her screaming at us from the sub. The tow line had somehow come undone, and the boat was no longer towing the sub. We would have to turn around to go get her, reattach the tow line, and then turn around again to continue on to the dock. The main problem was that we were in the narrow waterways of the marina, so maneuvering the boat was going to be quite tricky, especially with the slack tow line still trailing us in the water.

Then the bad situation took a turn for the worse.

The slow current was pushing the sub toward the marina's breakwater, and it would be only minutes before it would softly collide with the rocky wall. Typically, this would not be a huge issue, since the person on the sub could simply turn on the sub's power and use its thrusters to maneuver it to safety. Unfortunately, the person on the sub was a deckhand and not a trained sub pilot.

I asked the sub pilot riding in the boat to radio the deckhand on the sub and walk her through the thruster procedures. That is when I was informed that she did not have a radio on her. Fortunately, the sub pilot thought quickly and used his cell phone to call hers, so he was able to talk her through the process and avert a potential disaster.

From that point forward, we implemented two new safety measures. First, anyone who was alone on the sub needed to have a VHF radio for communications. Second, and much more importantly, we would never leave anyone on the sub without a trained pilot also on board.

This was not a major incident and no one was ever in any grave danger, but it was a potentially bad outcome that was completely avoidable. At least it helped improve our safety procedures without any real damage or personal injuries.

On another particular dive, we learned perhaps the most strategically significant lesson in OceanGate's history, with its importance resonating for over a decade, including *Titan*'s final dive.

As we conducted our various training dives in the dark murky depths of Puget Sound, we were often asked what we saw down there. It turned out that we really did not know what we saw, because none of us were scientists. As sub operators, we were not trained in oceanography, marine biology, nautical archaeology, or any other field that would help fulfill that drive that Stockton and I felt toward exploration for the purpose of scientific discovery. Also, none of us had the requisite scientific credentials to adequately fulfill the Coast Guard's requirements for an ORV operation.

So we decided to start bringing guest scientists on every training dive, and one of the first was the science director for the Seattle Aquarium. He was an experienced scuba diver and an expert in six-gilled sharks, which were resident in Puget Sound but difficult to study because of their propensity to live at depths greater than a scuba diver could attain. He was excited to join our dive and go beyond anywhere he had ever been.

The dive started in typical fashion, as we dropped quietly through the cold water and settled gently on the barren bottom about 600 feet (183 meters) below the surface. Per our protocol, I called up to the support boat while Stockton conducted safety checks, and we prepared to lift off and continue our dive. At that point, all hell broke loose from the forward dome where the scientist was sitting.

"Oh my god! Check this out! I can't believe it!"

From the pilot's seat in the middle of the sub, Stockton quickly leaned over the scientist's shoulder to see what he anticipated would be a potential safety risk. I was in the aft dome, so the best I could do was take a half-step and hunch over to Stockton's right. The scientist was pointing excitedly while also furiously snapping photos with his camera.

"What?" Stockton asked.

"That!"

"You mean that small ratfish?"

"It's not just a ratfish! It's a juvenile female ratfish!"

"Really? We see those down here all the time," said Stockton.

"Are you kidding me? That's incredible!"

Stockton and I were confused. Looking back, it was almost comical. We were disappointed, because based on his initial reaction, we thought that the scientist had discovered something really cool. Instead, he had found what our team usually called "just another ratfish."

For the rest of the dive and even during the post-dive debrief, the scientist went on and on about the symbiotic relationship between ratfish and six-gilled sharks, about their feeding patterns, about the mating habits of the ratfish, and many other topics that went way over all of our heads. There was a clear connection between the development of young ratfish—especially females—and the six-gilled sharks that this scientist had spent a big part of his career studying. Apparently, he had never seen a juvenile female ratfish because it was believed that they existed only at great depths. His effusive enthusiasm was contagious.

Stockton and I instantly decided that every one of our dives needed to have a scientist on board, or at least a subject-matter expert. This was the role that PH Nargeolet would later play on the crew of *Titan*'s final dive.

We hired a science coordinator to reach out to various scientists in order to offer them free dives in *Antipodes*. We knew that they did not have the budget to buy a new sub or perhaps even charter our sub, so we figured they would jump at the chance to collect data at depth. They would get a free dive, and we would get practice conducting science missions while also fulfilling our company's founding vision. It was a win-win situation.

We were shocked that very few scientists were interested in our offer.

It was not because of OceanGate, *Antipodes*, or even subs in general. They were all truly excited about that part of it. Rather, for them, the challenge was lack of funding for the data analysis. One researcher at the University of Washington showed us a storage facility with dozens of core samples from several past missions. She said that she did not have the budget to hire post-docs to analyze the samples, so they were just lying there waiting for someone to unlock their mysteries.

When Stockton and I had conducted our initial whiteboard session to develop OceanGate's founding vision, we had actually considered this as a potential problem we could try solving. Ultimately, we decided against it, because we thought it was more suitable for a nonprofit organization. However, in the aftermath of that first ratfish discovery, we revisited that possibility.

Since we had ultimately found equity investors for OceanGate as a for-profit venture, we had shifted our OceanGate Foundation toward marine education by awarding student scholarships. We were never truly comfortable with that mission, because there were already so many other ocean-focused nonprofits doing the same thing. We felt we had to pivot again, this time to helping marine researchers with funding for field expeditions using crewed submersibles.

For the next decade, OceanGate and the OceanGate Foundation would grow this strategic relationship.

OceanGate would provide subs and dive operations to researchers, and the OceanGate Foundation would provide them grants and fellowships to pay for their time. The foundation also weaved in its programs to inspire students through community outreach activities. Sometimes the foundation would even charter subs from OceanGate in order to support certain scientific missions or education programs, and sometimes OceanGate would donate seats on charter missions to the foundation's researchers or make its pilots available for the foundation's student outreach projects.

It proved to be a mutually beneficial relationship right through the last *Titanic* expedition.

Summer 2010

Everett, Washington

The Technology Adoption Curve—after we made the strategic decision to build our own subs, Stockton and I constantly discussed this, and it ultimately became part of our public narrative. It was our way of bringing outside innovation thinking into the stale submersible community. We were not just trying to innovate for the sake of innovation, but rather, we were forced to innovate in order for our business model to work and for us to achieve our company's long-term vision to open the oceans. It just happened that doing this would also completely disrupt the status quo.

Actually, our technology innovation regarding sub design was the third innovation we decided to pursue. The first was our business model, since chartering a sub would be so much less expensive than buying, owning, and operating a sub that it would greatly increase humanity's access to the deep oceans.

Our second innovation was also not technical but operational.

If the primary objective was to drive down the cost of access to the deep oceans, then we had to completely reevaluate the cost structure of traditional dive operations. The best way to make exponential cuts in costs was to focus on the largest cost factors. For submersibles, that was the fuel for the support ships.

One of the defining elements of a submersible is that it cannot operate independent of a surface support ship, on which it relies for transportation, crew transfers, recharging, maintenance, communications, and a host of other essential functions, depending on the dive mission profile. The standard practice was to place subs on the decks of big ships and then use the onboard cranes to put the subs in the water and retrieve them after their dives. As we had already analyzed, under this mode of operation, the best option was to use lighter subs that would require smaller cranes and therefore smaller ships using less fuel.

However, the further Stockton and I got into our own dive operations, the more confident we felt that we could reduce costs even further. If smaller cranes were good for reducing costs, then it seemed to us that eliminating cranes altogether would be even better. For a sub charterer like OceanGate, this would allow us to offer our subs for an even lower cost, thereby increasing the availability of subs to a much broader swath of humanity.

Our confidence was bolstered when we discovered that we were not the first sub operator to see this same opportunity. The University of Hawaii had already come up with an innovative way to avoid ship-based cranes altogether. They created a Launch, Retrieval, and Transportation system, or LRT. Their LRT model was essentially a flat sinkable barge that could be towed behind a relatively small boat, even in the open ocean.

They would use a marina-based crane to load their subs onto the floating platform and clamp it down. Once the integrated sub-and-LRT system arrived at the dive site, the crew would be loaded into the sub and the coupled system would dive to roughly 30 feet (about 10 meters), suspended there by its lines attached to buoys floating on the surface. This also provided crews with the additional benefit of performing delicate maneuvers below the water line and therefore below any waves, rough seas, or inclement weather.

From that stable depth, the sub would then decouple from the LRT, "lift off" the deck, and then proceed with its dive mission. When the dive was completed, the whole process would reverse, with the pilot "landing" the sub on the waiting, submerged, and stable deck. Once recoupled, the LRT would rise out of the water and float on the surface, at which point the crew would disembark and make its way back to the support boat.

The University of Hawaii used this LRT system for years. Not only did it bring their sub operations budget down to a manageable amount, but also it increased the safety of their dive operations. After all, subs that relied on traditional ship-based cranes required "swimmers" to jump into the water to attach the crane's hooks to the sub's pick-points. These were very risky maneuvers, especially in rough seas, and typically forced the support ship captain into a modified "man overboard" drill.

We believed that incorporating this type of LRT capability into OceanGate's operations would give us exactly the additional cost savings we needed to enhance our business model and improve our offerings to the ocean exploration community. Stockton connected with someone at the University of Hawaii, and they were generous enough to share with us their design specs and any support we needed.

We started building our own LRT system for *Antipodes*, and we continued iterating on its design and operations throughout the next decade. Each of our subs, including *Cyclops* and *Titan*, had its own mated LRT system, and we used them on expeditions throughout the United States, the Gulf of Mexico, the Bahamas, and ultimately the wreck of the *Titanic*.

Driving down operational costs was so mission-critical for OceanGate that we intentionally created a corporate culture around it. Every time we made a technical design or operations decision, we asked three questions:

1. Would this help improve safety?
2. Would this help achieve dive mission objectives?
3. Would this help reduce costs?

It was worth noting that we asked them in that particular order, because safety was always the top priority and would never be sacrificed for the good of the other two.

This culture led to some interesting results, even in the company's early days. Some were positive, some were not. And some were downright hilarious.

The most long-lasting example was our decision to use off-the-shelf game controllers for the subs, something we started experimenting with in *Antipodes*. As silly as it may have seemed to an outside observer, this was one idea that helped with all three concerns: safety, mission readiness, and costs.

When we first purchased *Antipodes*, it was outfitted with a legacy custom-built controller, which was a very heavy metal box attached to a side panel via a thick, cumbersome umbilical. On the top of the box were six three-position toggle switches. These were meant to control the sub's two vertical thrusters and four horizontal thrusters mounted one on each corner of the sub. The switches' three positions represented "forward," "reverse," and "neutral."

The sub pilot would have to envision all six thrusters and toggle the switches to make the sub go where the pilot wanted it to go. For example, to go straight forward, the pilot would flip the four horizontal thruster switches to their forward positions. Then to turn left, the switches for the two port horizontal thrusters would have to move into the neutral position. To coast, all four of the horizontal thruster switches would move into neutral, and to stop, all four would go to reverse until the sub's forward momentum had been cut, and then to neutral.

Needless to say, this was an incredibly cumbersome and arcane setup. Sub pilots would have to sit with the controller in their laps and place both hands on the box with six fingers stretched out across the six switches, three per hand. This was just for the thrusters, so it left no way for the pilots to also manage the ballast tanks, life support systems, sonar, navigation, and communications. It was uncomfortable, inefficient, and, worst of all, a safety risk.

And yet, this was accepted by ABS as being "in compliance with current industry standards." Stockton and I were appalled.

In order to fix this, we were told that we would have to hire a specialized electronics engineer to custom-build a new controller that would meet all of the current safety standards. We thought this was ridiculous.

Stockton took a different approach, thinking about this from his perspective as an aerospace engineer and as an airplane pilot. Since sub pilots were known to fly their subs underwater, why not use a more traditional "joystick" controller? This way the pilot would not need to worry about what each thruster was doing and only had to know what she wanted the sub to do, letting the controller do the rest. Airplanes had been doing this for so long that video game companies had already developed such controllers for flight simulation games. Also, these were mass-produced, which meant they were subjected to thorough testing for functionality and durability, they were available anywhere as replacement parts, and they were inexpensive. This seemed like such a no-brainer that even Stockton was ashamed to call it an "innovation."

We started with a simple joystick controller on *Antipodes*, and the results were drastic and immediate. As an additional benefit, we managed to convince ABS that we could list this as a minor improvement, because we had not changed anything about the electrical connections from the controller to the thrusters outside the protection of the pressure vessel. This allowed us to keep our current certificate from them.

Over the next ten years, this system evolved from using joysticks to using Xbox and PlayStation controllers, in part because they offered more capabilities but primarily because they were small, lightweight, wireless, and ultrareliable. This improved the efficiency of the pilots, the safety of the missions, and the enjoyment of the crew.*

Unsurprisingly, not all of our cost-cutting ideas were as successful as the LRT system and the game controllers. The most sadly hilarious was Stockton's infamous LED lights.

At one point, we decided that we needed to improve *Antipodes*' external lighting capabilities, so we wanted to add a strip of LED lights along the bottom guardrails protecting each of the sub's two hemispherical acrylic domes. One of the sub pilots I had tasked with this responsibility sourced a vendor that had exactly what we needed and asked for permission to make the purchase.

"Twenty-five hundred dollars? *Each*?" Stockton was shocked. "You just take a piece of plastic tubing, put some LEDs inside, fill it with oil, cap it on one end, and attach the wires on the other. That's like less than $10."

"Maybe," I said. "But we don't have time for all that. We're already overstretched with dive ops. Plus, this is a 'nice-to-have' and not mission-critical, so we can't afford the distraction."

---

* Years later, months after the accident, when the media skewered Stockton for using Xbox controllers on *Titan*, I took a tour of an older sub that had recently been completely refurbished. The owner, who had also personally conducted the overhaul, showed me how the thrusters were controlled by a joystick. When I asked him how they controlled the two manipulator arms, he smiled, reached behind a seat cushion, and tossed me an Xbox controller. Apparently, the classing agency had allowed it to be used for the exterior robotic arms because they were deemed "not mission critical" but not for the thrusters because they were "mission critical." However, the arms are much more complex to operate than the thrusters, so their assessment made no sense. We discussed that Stockton was probably a decade or so ahead of his time when it came to these types of innovations becoming industry standards.

"It can't possibly take that long. What? A couple of hours, start to finish, including the trip to the hardware store."

"Stockton, I know you're the engineer here, but I know that these projects never seem to go as smoothly as the engineers think."

"Fine, I'll do it."

"You don't have the time either," I pointed out.

"Don't worry. I've got a couple of hours. No problem."

Over the next few weeks, Stockton burned through countless iterations of his LED strips. For each one, we had to mount them on the sub and test them at depth during our training dives. They never worked, but Stockton was convinced that he could make it happen. What started as a small side project had morphed into a personal challenge. He was determined to see it through to the end.

One day, I was sitting at my desk when Stockton walked in.

"Screw it. Buy the damn lights."

He turned and left. We never discussed the lights again.

Of course, all of these were relatively minor technology innovations when compared to what we were planning for our new sub designs, specifically with the use of carbon fiber for the pressure hull. Our business model innovations and our operations model innovations did not require us to build our own subs. However, since none of the existing sub builders could meet our business requirements, we found ourselves forced to become technology innovators as well.

For this, Stockton decided to take a first-principles approach, starting with our most basic needs and assumptions, many of which conflicted with each other. We wanted to carry too many people to too great a depth with too much visibility in too light a vessel for too low a cost. As a nonengineer, the best I could do to help during these early brainstorming sessions was to challenge the assumptions on our business requirements. Did we really need to carry five people? Did we really need to go that deep? And so on.

Stockton wanted to find an engineering solution that would not require us to compromise on our founding vision. He conducted extensive research. He spoke with as many people as possible, from the sub community to shipbuilders, aircraft manufacturers, and car companies. He also looked at the world of robotics, including satellites, drones, and submersibles, such as remotely operated vehicles and autonomous underwater vessels. No idea was too crazy to be discarded outright. While I worked with the team to hone our dive operations with *Antipodes*, Stockton spent countless hours immersing himself in the pursuit of this final piece of our puzzle.

Over time, he became convinced that the two most limiting factors were the form of the hull (which constrained the crew capacity and the transportability) and the material of the hull (which increased the weight and the cost). He started looking at cylindrical designs (like *Antipodes*) made of alternative materials such as carbon fiber (like Graham's *DeepFlight Challenger*). We came up with a plan to take these ideas to the next level and raised some more equity capital.

All of this brings us back to the Technology Adoption Curve.

This was usually depicted as a standard bell curve. The common thinking was that customers adopted new technologies along a fairly normal distribution. On the far end of the curve was a small minority of innovators, who were always ready and eager to try the newest technologies. At the opposite end were the laggards, who would likely never be convinced to switch to anything new and would do so only when forced to do so by outside factors. Right next to the innovators were the early adopters, who were willing to try new things but did not feel the need to be first. Finally, in the meaty part of the curve were the early majority and the late majority, who basically sat on a spectrum, depending on how much they needed a new technology to be proven or to come down in price before adopting them.

This graphical framework was used for almost all technologies, from software to automobiles to video games to airplanes to consumer electronics. Stockton and I used it to create the final piece of our innovation model.

We founded the company with the ambitious goal of creating a sub-diving business that would help humanity explore the world's oceans. To accomplish this, we had to develop a matrix of three interlocking innovations: (1) our charter business model, (2) our LRT-based operations model, and (3) our carbon fiber deep-diving submersibles. We used the Technology Adoption Curve to try answering the most basic business question: Who was going to pay for all of this?

After a fair amount of market research and many discussions with agency officials, company executives, and service providers, we convinced ourselves that the bulk of the market (i.e., the early majority and the late majority) were most likely going to be in the energy sector and in the national security sector. That is not why

Stockton and I got into this business, but that was most likely the best path for our investors to gain a financial return. We would have to "de-risk" the whole solution before we could approach them, but our early conversations with them gave us confidence that the market demand would be there when we were ready.

The rationale for the energy sector was based on its historical experience with submersible operations.

In the 1960s and early 1970s, energy companies relied on crewed submersibles to establish oil drilling operations on the ocean floor. It was risky and expensive, but it got the job done. As underwater robots became more capable in the 1970s, they replaced humans as a way of driving down risk and cost. Over the next few decades, these robots got more capable and they operated deeper, increasing their complexity and size. These were tethered to a surface ship, where a pilot would control them. As the vehicles got bigger and went deeper, their tethers also got bigger and longer, which in turn led to larger surface ships that burned more fuel. Taken altogether, these developments created a situation of skyrocketing costs for underwater robotic operations. Even worse, they got riskier, as unexpected weather conditions could completely destroy billions of dollars' worth of sensitive equipment.

The people we spoke with in the industry told us that everything had come full circle. While robots had replaced humans in the 1970s due to risk and cost, it was entirely possible that humans could come back to replace robots for the same reasons.

The rationale for the defense sector was quite different and based on two divergent perceived threats to national security.

The one that made occasional media headlines was the use of submersibles by drug cartels to smuggle their contraband into US waters. The other, lesser-known one was the fear that the Russian and Chinese militaries might develop small submersible recon and first-strike capabilities in order to bypass American defense systems designed to combat large submarines. In both cases, members of the Defense Department, US Coast Guard, Customs and Border Patrol, and various law enforcement agencies contacted us for help. It was never clear to me or Stockton what they might want from us, but it was certainly clear that there was interest in our future deep-diving subs.

That was the bulky middle of the Technology Adoption Curve, but to get there we would have to start with the innovators and early adopters.

For submersibles, those tended to be adventurers, explorers, scientists, storytellers, and tourists. Of those, Stockton and I were most philosophically aligned with the explorers and scientists, with storytellers coming along to help build inspirational connections, much like Jacques Cousteau had. We were happy to leave the wealthy recreational crowd and the tourist operations to the existing sub builders.

So the question remained: How could we gain initial traction with explorers, scientists, and storytellers who wanted to use our subs for the deep oceans?

We came across a feature story about a nonprofit organization called EarthWatch that ran "citizen scientist" programs with archaeologists. They offered other expeditions, but the story that caught our attention was about their archaeology projects. People would pay to join an archaeological dig and then spend days toiling in the dirt, helping researchers with their field studies. More importantly, from a business perspective, they would pay a premium to do this. The rationale was that they were subsidizing the researchers' field expeditions while also doing something unique, meaningful, and fulfilling. In other words, they were paying for the experience rather than for the trip.

Stockton and I jumped on this. We had absolutely no desire to run a tourism business. However, if we could find a way of bringing together ocean scientists with wealthy philanthropic donors for the common purpose of exploration expeditions, then perhaps we could prove out the next deep subs we were designing and potentially even subsidize their development. And if we were talking about scientists and donors, would it make more sense to have the OceanGate Foundation do this, and then it could simply charter the OceanGate subs for the expeditions? Better yet, could we find an existing tour operator who might be willing to embrace such a model and charter our subs for its expeditions?

The fact that our subs were designed to carry five crew members made it especially easy to accommodate this type of model. With one pilot and one scientist on board, we would still have room for up to three citizen scientists. We decided that this term was not appropriate, because not everyone would want to work with the scientists and might prefer to work with us as sub operators. Instead, Stockton and I reached into our space backgrounds and decided that the term "Mission Specialists" made more sense, since it would give them flexibility to participate in almost any aspect of a dive mission. Also, this had the added benefit of helping us comply with US Coast Guard ORV regulations if we ever wanted to operate in US waters.

We had early conversations with several tour operators to gauge their level of interest. They were certainly intrigued, but most of them needed us to first prove it would work, both from a sub operations perspective and also from a financial and market demand perspective. Even though we did not want to go into the tourism business, we felt that the best way to attack the Technology Adoption Curve would be to try the Mission Specialist model.

We started testing this approach with *Antipodes*, but it really took hold with *Cyclops* before maturing into the *Titanic* expeditions program.

Chapter 7

TROLLS

Summer 2023

Atlanta, Georgia

"OceanGate Cofounder Slams Cameron." That headline appeared above trifold images of James Cameron on the left and me on the right, facing each other, with *Titan* in between.

"I did *what*?" I yelled to my girlfriend.

From across the room, she held out her phone so I could see the story. *Crap!*

"Did I really come across as slamming him?" I asked.

"No," she said. "And actually, the story itself gets everything right. You said that he was one of the most experienced ocean explorers, sub designers, and sub pilots. You said that you respected him and his opinion. Then you said that your only problem was that he had no direct evidence, that he was just speculating like everyone else, and that he should wait until the investigations are finished to weigh in."

"So the headline just didn't match the story?" I asked.

"Exactly."

I sat at my laptop to scan various other headlines, and I found exactly what my girlfriend had already discovered. Some of them were accurate, but most of them were clearly clickbait. In fact, many of the latter had nothing to do with the actual content of the story and even contradicted the content of the story, just like that Cameron piece. It was clear that the headlines and the stories were created by two different people, each with a different objective. This was frustrating but not unexpected.

In the days following the media frenzy, I was left to assess the damage to my life. I felt like someone returning to their home after a hurricane, tornado, flood, earthquake, or wildfire. It was still a bit early to fully determine how much harm I had inflicted upon myself, but the initial review was not promising.

The media outlets with which I had conducted interviews were not that bad. They acted as I expected, and so the results were as I anticipated. Every journalist with whom I interacted was courteous, respectful, and professional. Their questioning clearly pushed me in a direction they had predetermined based on their chosen narrative. However, they appreciated that I understood they had a job to do, so they all gave me leeway to express my core messages. The live interviews were as fair as possible, even if the recorded interviews got cut down to a few well-placed sound bites. I did not have a problem with anyone I spoke with, because they were trying as hard as possible to adhere to their code of journalistic integrity.

However, I did take issue with two categories of media.

The first were what I called the "me too" or "copycat" outlets. They did not interview me. Instead, they waited for someone else to publish their story based on an interview I gave, and then they pilfered selected segments of that story and rearranged them to publish them as their own. They did just enough to avoid charges of plagiarism, but I knew they were stolen because they were sloppy enough to also change my quotes. The worst part was that it turned into a game of telephone. Every interview, no matter how thorough the journalist, yielded stories with at least some errors, mostly minor but with an occasional major one slipping through. Since the copycat outlets did not know which were accurate and which were not, when they copy-and-pasted the lines into their stories and embellished, their stories typically came out as complete farces. To make matters worse to the point of being comical, some copycat outlets would plagiarize other copycat outlets, so the errors would amplify exponentially.

My favorite example came from the first interview I gave a couple of weeks after the accident where the journalist inquired about my current work with the Humans2Venus Foundation. That nonprofit organization supports Venus-focused science and engineering programs, with a long-term vision of establishing a permanent human presence of 1,000 people in the Venusian atmosphere by the year 2050. The actual viability of this effort is irrelevant for the purposes of this discussion. What matters is that the original journalist, who was the science editor at a major media outlet, posted the story and was incredibly fair and accurate in her article. Her headline read something like "OceanGate Co-Founder Wants 1,000 People to Live in Venus's Atmosphere." Unsurprisingly, that headline and article got picked up and picked apart by a slew of copycat outlets. After a few iterations, I came across a headline that read something like "After Killing 5 Billionaires Underwater, OceanGate Now Wants to Land 1,000 Billionaires on Venus."

One of my favorite mantras is "When things are bad, they're bad, but when they get really bad, they're funny." Reading some of the ridiculous headlines, I just had to laugh.

Of course, the problem for me was that most people in today's society were not reading past the headlines and were not questioning whether they were true or accurate. Even if they did, they were not taking the time to do a little research to educate themselves. That was exactly what the copycats were counting on. And that was exactly what would wreak havoc on my personal and professional life.

I felt petty and even ashamed for caring about any of this when I knew that there were four families mourning the loss of their loved ones and a whole team of OceanGate employees coping with the tragedy. My problems were minuscule when put in that context, especially because they were self-inflicted. Still, they were problems I had to face.

As expected, the worst of the worst were the trolls on social media.

It did not even dawn on me before I jumped into the public discussion that a global media frenzy of this magnitude would yield an exponentially larger explosion of backlash on social media. Looking back, it was a gross oversight on my part, but it probably would not have changed my mind. Still, I was shocked by the sheer volume of ignorant hate, filth, and venom that spewed forth from every dark corner of the internet.

As disgusting as it was, it did not seem to bother me personally. After all, I was not on social media that much, and besides, most of it was so extreme that it was laughable. Flipping through social media comments mostly just made me sad for humanity, because all I kept thinking about was how low modern civilization had sunk.

More importantly, being the primary target of such a vast social media attack gave me a new appreciation for how difficult it was to be a journalist in today's society. As I mentioned, every journalist that I spoke with was courteous, respectful, and professional. They showed compassion and sympathy for my loss before and after going on the air, and they maintained proper decorum during our interviews. They were clearly trying as much as possible to adhere to their code of journalistic integrity. They treated me with respect, and I reciprocated in kind.

However, they all worked for companies that had to make money in order to survive, so they had to remember to please their audiences in order to support their sponsors and advertisers. They knew what their viewers, listeners, and readers wanted, and they very deftly maneuvered me into whatever direction they needed me to go. I did not fault them for this because it was reality, and to expect otherwise would have been naive of me. Regardless, I felt that they tried their best to remain focused on communicating the truth, even if they took some liberties with which truths they presented, what order they presented them in, and in what manner they presented them.

At the other end of the spectrum was social media, trolls or otherwise.

As I already knew from watching it grow over the years from

its inception, this online world had no rules, no guardrails, and certainly no code of ethics. Anyone could post anything they wanted anywhere they wanted at any time they wanted. Nothing needed sources, and nothing needed to be fact-checked. Worse, there seemed to be millions of people around the world willing to ingest this drivel, blindly accept it as truth, and then spread it to everyone in their networks.

This was the opponent that journalists were facing.

Not too long ago, journalists rushed to print in order to avoid getting "scooped" by other journalists. Since all of the journalists were playing by the same rules, the best journalists were the ones who could work quickly yet maintain their journalistic integrity by conducting proper research and double-checking reliable sources. Nowadays, they risk getting scooped by social media, which operates without such cumbersome limitations. They play two completely different games, but sadly, audiences cannot tell the difference. Hence the dawn of "fake news." This was the tension that I felt even as I was going through the gauntlet of interviews.

To make matters worse for me, social media was much more important to my three kids than to me, so they experienced much more of the backlash than I did. Or at least they were exposed to much more of it than I was.

After the news cycle shifted and I saw a lull in my interview schedule, my girlfriend and I made an unplanned trip back to Atlanta. I wanted to see my kids and talk through the whole experience with them. They had known Stockton and had dived in *Antipodes*, so this hit very close to home. I needed to make sure they were okay, and I needed them to know that I was okay, too. Thankfully, they were strong enough to withstand the onslaught and intelligent enough to see the trolls for what they were. It was the only silver lining in an otherwise bleak ten days.

I was not sure what the future would hold for me or how much more fallout there would be from my decision to insert myself into the global media circus. I had survived the first week. I knew this was just the beginning, and it would likely get worse before it got better. For now, there was a quiet period.

And that was when it really hit me.

Stockton was gone.

Chapter 8

EXPEDITIONS AND SAFETY

Summer 2010

Catalina Island, California

IT WAS TIME TO TAKE IT UP A NOTCH. WE KNEW THAT EVENTUALLY WE would have to be proficient enough to ship our team and subs anywhere in the world, so we needed to get out of the Seattle area and try operating in the open ocean. We practiced taking our operations on the road by doing a mini expedition to Port Townsend, just across Puget Sound from our home base in Everett, and then we felt we were ready. As a next baby step, we decided to stay in US waters but head down the West Coast to Catalina Island, just off the coast of Southern California.

We were scheduled to spend six weeks diving around the island, but it was cut short after the second week. We learned two critical lessons on safety.

By the time the sub and team arrived in Catalina, we had already developed a robust set of safety measures, processes, and protocols in Seattle. Some of these were industry norms, but most of them were either borrowed from other industries or the byproduct of an anomaly during one of our training exercises.

Humans tend to learn better from failures than from successes, which was why Stockton and I had intentionally created a corporate culture that depended on open communication, regular pre- and post-dive briefs, and detailed documentation of every single anomaly, no matter how small. Having experienced other sub operations firsthand, I knew that ours went above and beyond industry best practices. Then again, we knew that our reputation for safety would be a key element to our ultimate success as a sub charterer, more so than for any other sub operator.

We were draconian about basic safety measures like ensuring that everyone wore close-toed shoes while working, that everyone put on PFDs (personal flotation devices) while on the water and even at the dock when getting on and off the boat or sub, and that everyone in the vicinity of a functioning crane wore a construction hard hat. These seemed like common sense, but I was shocked by how many other ship and sub operators would ignore them.

Stockton also insisted that all expeditions use "dry" ships, meaning no alcohol on board. Even though he did not drink, he acknowledged that others might want to, and generally he trusted people to act like adults and not abuse it. However, he had two valid reasons for imposing this requirement. The first was that our role as a sub charterer meant that we would always have non-OceanGate crew members on board—presumably our clients—and while he trusted our team, he was wary of the risk new strangers might pose. "Better safe than sorry," as he would say. The second was that the ocean was an unforgiving environment, prone to sudden shifts in weather and sea conditions. No one ever knew when they might unexpectedly be thrust into a critical role during an emergency situation. He reasoned that there was never a "safe" time to have a drink while underway.

Stockton was the primary driver behind some of our earliest sub operations safety protocols, leaning heavily into his background as an airplane pilot and his personal interest in human spaceflight. We developed a series of checklists for just about every aspect of our operations, from shipping and storage, to launch and retrieval, to towing and diving, to maintenance and repair, to communications and crisis management. His mind worked fast, so he had to make sure that he did not miss anything critical. We needed everyone else to do the same.

Every member of the team was expected not only to adhere to our safety protocols and call out any observed violations, but also to actively contribute to the development of these protocols. My personal favorite was the brainstorm of one of our early directors of marine operations, a seasoned mariner with decades of experience on a wide range of boats and ships around the world.

At one point, he decided that everyone on the team should cleat lines ("ropes" for boats) in the exact same way, mostly just in case anyone had to quickly uncleat a line during an emergency. A cleat is a wood or metal anchor that is fixed on a dock, so that boats can tie lines to them when mooring. The most common are horn cleats, which are shaped generally like anvils, with two "horns" extending out from the base, parallel to the edge of the dock. Lines are typically secured using a cleat hitch knot, but there are many variations.

Our director of marine operations noticed that almost everyone on our team was using a different variation of the cleat hitch knot. He also noticed that almost everyone on our team was having trouble uncleating lines that had been cleated by others because the knot had not been secured the same way they would have done it. He considered this a potential safety hazard, since it could cause problems in situations where a line needed to be uncleated quickly. Therefore, on his own initiative, he decided that everyone should use the exact same knot, and he conducted a training session where he taught everyone the same way to tie the cleat hitch knot. From that day forward, every new member of the OceanGate team was trained on how to properly cleat a line "the OceanGate way."

Perhaps one of the most significant safety measures was the culture Stockton cultivated among the sub pilots for attention to detail.

During every dive operation, the sub pilot was expected to keep track of every single anomaly, no matter how minute or insignificant it might seem. After every dive, the last task the pilot had to complete before checking out was to transfer all of those notes into a dive log and a maintenance log. This would take a long time, even for someone moving as fast as Stockton. Conversely, the first task for any sub pilot before a dive was to review the dive log and the maintenance log—not just the items from the previous dive, but the *entire* log. The pilot needed to ensure that every noted item had been closed/resolved, and that the pilot was aware of every noted item that was still open/unresolved. Again, no anomaly was too small to escape this process. (During a pre-dive log review, I once noted an open item that the "air freshener ran out," which referred to a small container of scented pellets that the sub pilot would subtly open during a dive if one of the crew members had smelly socks or body odor.)

There were serious reasons for driving such attention to detail on anomalies. The most obvious was that something might seem inconsequential to one person but turn out to be immensely critical to another. Also, a minor anomaly might be an indicator of a much greater problem, which might not manifest itself until later. More philosophically, Stockton wanted to make sure that everyone, and especially the sub pilots, was comfortable admitting that something had not worked exactly like it was supposed to. After all, there would always be something that failed on a dive mission. It was the nature of operating in such a hostile environment.

In Catalina, we were learning all sorts of lessons from our training dives.

It was our first time operating so far from our home base and outside the protected waters of Puget Sound. While this presented many new operational challenges, it was nice to be on the open water with little to no boat traffic to contend with on the surface. Also, the sub pilots were loving the crystal clear Pacific Ocean water that allowed so much sunlight to get through that we often did not even turn on our exterior lights even at 800 feet (245 meters). In retrospect, the murky waters of Puget Sound—where we generally lost sunlight in the first 50 feet (15 meters)—had turned out to be an excellent training ground for pilots to become proficient with our sonar rather than relying on the views through the sub's twin hemispherical acrylic domes.

Once the team got settled in Catalina, Stockton flew down from Seattle and joined us for a few days of diving.

During his first dive, as we were flying level about 10 feet (3 meters) off the bottom, he noticed that the sub suddenly started pulling to starboard. He tried compensating, but the pulling got worse. He set the sub down and quickly started checking every system—the thrusters, the batteries, the electrical panels inside the sub. Everything. But he could not find anything wrong. He lifted the sub off the bottom and tried going forward again, but again the sub pulled right. He started getting agitated and set the sub down again. He could not figure out what was wrong. He told me to call up to the surface and let them know that we were going to sit tight while we fixed whatever was wrong. Then he pulled out the tool kit and started to disassemble the side panels and trace every wire. He was working lightning fast, and, as his co-pilot, I was trying my best to keep up.

The minutes ticked by, and he started getting more and more anxious. He wanted to continue the dive. He was convinced that someone else had broken something during one of the prior test dives, even though there was nothing in the logs and I assured him that the sub had been working perfectly. I was not sure why we had taken off the side panels, since that was something we really should not have to do during a dive. According to our safety protocols, we should have simply aborted the dive, come to the surface, and assessed the situation there or back on the dock. But Stockton did not want to do that; he wanted to finish the dive. I would not say that he was frantic, but it was certainly the most "not calm" I had ever seen him during a dive.

In the midst of the mayhem, Scott Cassell offered whatever assistance and advice he could.

A former member of the special forces, he was not only an expert scuba diver but also a sub pilot with over eight hundred sub dives under his belt. He had created a nonprofit organization to help save shark populations around the world, and we had become friends who shared a mutual passion for the oceans and subs. He and I especially clicked due to our shared military backgrounds, even though he was far more experienced than I was. The two of us had already conducted several dives together in *Antipodes*, and I truly respected his poise and grace under pressure. This was his first dive with Stockton.

He was now crouching in the forward dome, pointing off into the distance.

"Uh, guys. You might want to check this out."

Stockton stood up in the conning tower, and I went to the aft dome. Both of us looked in the direction of where Scott was pointing, and in an instant the mystery was solved.

For several reasons, we had been diving with a buoy trailing us on the end of a 100-foot (30-meter) line that was attached to the deck on top of the sub. Off to our right were a few abandoned crab pots resting on the bottom. One of them had a buoy attached to it by a line that was maybe 200 feet (60 meters) long. It had been floating directly above the crab pot. At least until we flew right past it and caught its line with ours.

Our buoy line was tangled with the crab pot's buoy line. That was why we were pulling around into a clockwise circle.

"I bet if we just back up, then we'll just untangle and get free."

I knew Scott was right, and so did Stockton. Sure enough, it worked. In less than a minute, we were clear of the entanglement, and *Antipodes* was back to normal. We reattached the side panel, put away the tool kit, called up to the surface with the good news, and continued the dive. All thanks to Scott staying calm and properly assessing the situation.

This was a huge lesson learned for us. Stockton had always told all crew members and sub pilots that the most important thing to do in an emergency was to stay calm. Unlike in airplanes, where pilots had to make quick decisions to avoid potential disasters, everything in a sub moved slowly, so there was no reason to rush. In fact, the only situation that required quick actions from the sub pilot was a fire, since a key element of the life support system was to pump pure oxygen into the sub. Otherwise, pilots could take their time and calmly assess any situation.

On that dive, Stockton had violated his own cardinal rule.

It turned out to be a minor incident, but it was a clear lesson that we passed on to all crew members and sub pilots.

The irony was that Scott Cassell had also been in the sub when we had a fault with our underwater radio during a training dive in Puget Sound a few weeks before the Catalina expedition. On that dive, I was the pilot and Stockton was in the support boat as Mission Director. When we first descended, we followed our protocol with a radio check upon landing on the bottom. We could hear the communications from the support boat, but they could not hear us, so we did not know if that was a problem with our transmitter or with their receiver. Scott asked what our protocol was for lost comms. I explained that the comms log on the boat would reflect our missed comm, and they would try again to contact us in fifteen minutes. If that failed, they would log it and try again in another fifteen minutes. If that failed, they would try one final time in another fifteen minutes and then call the local Coast Guard sector for emergency assistance.

Since the sub was operating perfectly except for this singular communications issue and since we could hear the support boat letting us know that they were tracking us, Scott and I figured we had forty-five minutes to continue with our mission plan before we had to surface so Stockton would not have to call the Coast Guard. We proceeded according to that plan and broke the surface right at the forty-five-minute mark.

When we established communications with the boat via our VHS surface radio, it was clear that Stockton had never been worried and simply kept the crew following our emergency protocols for missed communications. Even though he was ready to call the Coast Guard, he was confident that we would surface according to the timelines in our safety protocols and instructed the crew to watch for us coming up.

I got the sense that even Scott was impressed with how well the entire crew handled that technical anomaly.

While the entanglement with the crab pot buoy line was a minor issue, a few days later in Catalina we experienced the most extreme incident in the history of our young company.

We had arranged for a few VIP researchers to join us for a couple of dives, and we wanted to impress them with a flawless operation.

The day before, we conducted a test dive at the target location, and sure enough, everything went smoothly. We were ready.

After pulling the sub out of the water, Stockton took a boat back to our shore headquarters to greet the scientists and host a dinner reception in their honor. I stayed behind with the other sub pilots to charge the sub, put it back in the water, and secure it for an overnight stay. Then we joined everyone else for the evening festivities.

Early the next morning, I took a boat out to the sub with the other pilots in order to prepare the sub for a full day of diving. Stockton was scheduled to follow us an hour later in a second boat with the researchers and the rest of the ops team. As we pulled up to the sub, we noticed that the sub was listing to port. I got a sick feeling in the pit of my stomach. I could think of only two causes for that list. One was minor and fixable, and one was major and catastrophic.

We pulled up to the dock. While the others secured the boat, I walked to the sub and hesitated as I opened the hatch. I heard the alarm going off inside, and I instantly knew what had gone wrong. Major and catastrophic, indeed.

After turning off the alarm and double-checking everything, we all confirmed what we all feared: The port battery pod was flooded. The water inside the pod had triggered the alarm in the crew compartment.

Antipodes was fitted with two long steel tubes running along its length, one on either side at the bottom of its cylindrical hull. They were approximately 1.5 feet (45 centimeters) wide and 18 feet (5.5 meters) long. Inside, they each contained a sliding rack of ten 12-volt batteries, collectively acting as two 120-volt battery pods, one port and one starboard. The sub typically used one for dive operations and kept the other as a redundant emergency reserve. They were sealed tight to keep the batteries dry.

That morning, the port pod was filled with water, which is why the sub was listing. Not only were we going to have to cancel the day's dives, but also we would likely have to cancel the rest of the expedition. The batteries were certainly damaged beyond repair with the influx of salty sea water, and replacing them was going to take longer than the time we had left in Catalina. While it would be possible to dive with only one pod, operating without a reserve power supply was a clear safety violation and not something we wanted to attempt.

None of us wanted to make the phone call, but I had to do it. Stockton was in disbelief and curtly hung up on me. In a few minutes, one of the other ops team members messaged me that he had rushed everyone (including the scientists) onto the second boat and was driving at breakneck speed to our location.

As he pulled the boat toward the dock, he turned over control to another member of our ops team and hopped across onto the dock while the boat was still moving. I did not want to point out that obvious safety violation, because clearly he was angry beyond anything I had ever seen from him. Without saying a word, he jogged across the dock in his swimsuit and carrying a mask. He was focused on *Antipodes*. He threw on the mask and jumped in the water, wanting to inspect the pod himself. It did not take long for him to surface.

"The damn cap on the release valve is missing!"

He told me to get the researchers to shore, so someone could drive them by car back to our shore headquarters in case we needed both boats. The dives were canceled, so they would have to go home. As I drove four of them in the dinghy, one of them said, "I didn't realize that this was such a life-threatening emergency."

"It's not. What do you mean?"

"The way Stockton reacted. It seems really serious. Could the sub explode or something?"

I suddenly realized that Stockton's actions were so dramatic that they were obvious even to researchers who had never met him. Our team had clearly never seen him act like this, but I thought that was just in comparison to how calm he usually was. Apparently, the scientists noticed it, too.

By the time I got our guests set for their return trip home and made my way back to the dock, Stockton and the other sub pilots had managed to get *Antipodes* out of the water. We removed the end cap on the port battery pod and watched in agony as gallons of sea water poured out of the tube. We pulled the rack out and tested the batteries. As expected, they were all fried.

Stockton was furious, but he did not know where to direct his anger. After all, nothing he could do at that point would change the fact that our Catalina expedition was ruined. We started making plans for closing up shop and getting back to Seattle.

Before anything else, we conducted a thorough investigation and debrief to figure out what had gone wrong. As typically happens in these catastrophic situations, it was the cumulative effect of three or four unconnected and otherwise benign events. However, the primary culprit was me.

The previous afternoon, I had been the senior sub pilot on the dock, so I had conducted the prelaunch inspection, and I had cleared the sub to be put back in the water. It had been my responsibility to ensure that the cap was on that release valve, and I had missed it. How that cap was removed in the first place and why none of the other sub pilots saw it was missing were contributing factors, but ultimately completely harmless. I should have caught the anomaly before giving the go-ahead.

My mistake cost us $5,000 to replace the batteries and other parts inside the pod. More importantly, it cost us the rest of the expedition.

The silver lining was that it had not been a dangerous failure. If it had happened during a dive, it would have been worse, mostly because we would have had to abort the dive and conduct a crew transfer at sea. However, it would still not have been anything life-threatening, since losing a battery pod during a dive was such an anticipated issue that the sub actually carried a redundant pod. Also, the additional weight of a flooded pod would not be sufficient to prevent the sub from surfacing, since clearly it merely caused it to list awkwardly to one side.

At least we learned critical safety lessons that we incorporated into our prelaunch checklist and protocols as well as our maintenance and repair processes.

However, as the company's CEO, my biggest concern was the impression that Stockton's overly dramatic reaction had left on the rest of the team. Maybe they had not noticed. Maybe they did not think it was that bad. Maybe it was just my perception because I was self-conscious about having caused the mishap and because until that moment, I had always considered him a bastion of calmness.

Regardless, while I still greatly respected and trusted Stockton, my unequivocal confidence in him had cracked just a little that day.

Spring 2011
Everett, Washington

I LIKED THE THREE-PHASE APPROACH. AS SOON AS WE MADE THE DECISION to add sub-building capabilities to our charter business, Stockton and I came up with a new long-term plan for OceanGate.

The first phase was our startup phase, which was primarily focused on dive operations. We were already into that phase with *Antipodes*. The second would be our R&D phase, when we would develop our new sub designs and put the deep sub into operations. The final phase would be our expansion phase, when we would complete our fleet of subs and expand charter operations around the world.

Along with that phased approach, we came up with a succession plan. Since I had more startup leadership and field operations experience, I would continue heading up the company during the first phase. Since Stockton was the engineer, he would take over during the second phase. For the third phase, we would likely bring on a professional "hired gun" CEO to manage and grow the business internationally.

Stockton and I were both comfortable with the phased strategy and with the succession plan. The only outstanding question would be the timing of everything, and we would have to play that by ear and make decisions as we went. In the meantime, we would continue evolving our twin pillars of dive operations under my leadership and sub design under Stockton's.

Seattle was proving to be an ideal place for the design work, since Stockton was able to develop early relationships with the University of Washington and Boeing. However, when it came to dive operations, we wanted to find a new home base that was better suited than Puget Sound. It did not have the best weather, and its remote location made it difficult to go on expeditions.

I spent weeks assessing various candidate targets, and ultimately we decided on Miami, figuring that the South Florida weather and proximity to the Bahamas would afford us greater opportunities to expand our dive capabilities. I would relocate my family to Florida, which would hopefully make Julie happy since she had family there. We would bring some of our ops team and hire more people when we got there. Stockton would stay in the Pacific Northwest, continuing to work on new sub designs and building our network of strategic partners. It would be risky to split our small team at such a critical stage of our company's development, but we felt it was the best path forward.

We had planned an expedition to Monterey, California, for the fall, so we decided to hold off until January for the big move. In a few months, OceanGate was scheduled to experience a shocking transition.

Fall 2011

Monterey, California

I COULD NOT BELIEVE WE WERE REALLY GOING TO DO THIS. WE WERE about to violate so many of our own self-imposed safety rules. Why? Just to accommodate the hectic schedule of a high-profile

VIP? I did not agree with the decision, though I could understand Stockton's risk analysis.

There were two primary reasons why we both wanted David Mayer de Rothschild to join our board of directors. We did not really need or want his family's money, and his famous last name could arguably become more of a liability than an asset. We also did not intend to leverage his network of contacts.

The main reason we wanted him on OceanGate's board was his personal commitment to environmental conservation and to protecting the world's oceans. As we took on investors, Stockton and I had developed a strategic business plan that would ultimately have us chartering subs to the energy sector and doing business with the national security community. While we believed that this was the best path for our investors, it was not why Stockton and I had started the company. In a very real way, we wanted someone on our board to be the "watchdog of our souls," just to make sure that we did not completely lose our moral compass along the path to financial success.

The second reason was his proven track record as an explorer, which resonated deeply with me and Stockton. Even though he was just in his early thirties, he had already conducted several successful expeditions in the Arctic and Antarctic regions. More relevant to OceanGate, he had been named one of National Geographic's Emerging Explorers in large part as a result of his Pacific crossing in *Plastiki*, a boat built using over 12,000 plastic bottles in order to raise public awareness about the Pacific Garbage Patch.

Not only was he an explorer at heart, but also he knew firsthand the wonder and power of the world's oceans.

Also, even though he and I never spoke about this specifically, I believe that Stockton saw a bit of himself in David. Perhaps a younger version of Richard Stockton Rush III? Someone born into a privileged family with a famous last name and the ancestral lineage to match. Someone hungry for adventure and the lure of exploration. Someone with a passion for the oceans and for helping humanity improve itself. Most importantly, someone whose personal passions chafed against the constraints of the revered family structure. A fellow "rich maverick."

David would be an ideal addition to OceanGate's board of directors, so Stockton and I pledged to do whatever it took to recruit him.

As an ocean advocate and explorer, David was naturally drawn to the core of our business—namely, submersibles. He was enthralled by the idea of going deeper than was possible using scuba equipment. He wanted a dive in the sub, and we were happy to oblige.

Given his heavy international travel schedule, it was nearly impossible to coordinate an overlap with our diving schedule. Then we found an opportunity during our expedition to Monterey. He and his girlfriend would be in California at roughly the same time as we would be diving *Antipodes*, so we started making arrangements for them to join us for a day of diving.

We went through our normal mission planning process and got everything set up. However, due to a last-minute change of plans in their travel itineraries, it turned out that David and his girlfriend would have only a few hours on the ground when they would be available. They asked if we could still fit them in just for three hours of diving, instead of a full day. Stockton replied yes, but then it fell to the rest of the team to figure out how to make it happen. It would not be trivial, and it would involve a fair amount of risk.

We worked backward from the ultimate objective of giving them a full sub dive experience in only three hours. We could not simply "dunk" them just outside the marina, in part because that would be only 50 feet (15 meters) and in part because that would not be exploration. Instead, we had to figure out how to get them into one of the many deep canyons just offshore. This is what caused the complexity and risk.

Given their time constraints, they could not be with us during the tow-out to the dive site; they would have to meet the sub there. Essentially, they would have to drive to the marina, get out of their car and step onto a speed boat, take the boat out to the dive site, board the sub, conduct the dive, and then reverse the process when they finished. It would be the quickest turnaround we had ever conducted.

Technically, it was not impossible. In fact, arguably, it made the process much easier since the bulk of the operation would be done by just the core OceanGate team. As long as they relayed to us beforehand each of their weights and the weight of the bags or equipment they wanted to carry inside the sub, we could make sure *Antipodes* was properly ballasted and ready to dive when they arrived. None of this was risky.

What made me nervous were the many steps we were stripping out of our typical process.

Over time, we had honed protocols for introducing guests to *Antipodes*, giving them a tour from outside and inside, ideally before launching it into the water but definitely dockside at the marina. We needed them to be familiar with the sub and to have opportunities to ask questions. We needed them to develop a rapport with their sub pilot. We needed them to learn about our at-sea plans, especially the crew transfers on and off the sub. And we needed them to be familiar with our emergency procedures and protocols.

More importantly, our team needed time to assess them, their demeanor, and their concerns. If they were going to get claustrophobic or nervous during the dive, it was better to know that beforehand. If they had a cold or an upset stomach, it was better to make a go/no-go decision on shore. If they had a broken arm or sprained ankle, it was better to assess their mobility before trying a maneuver on the open ocean.

Finally, although not absolutely critical, we needed to confirm their weights on shore. It still baffled us that people would always lie about their weights, even when we told them that accuracy was necessary for safe dive operations and that we would be weighing everyone before boarding the sub.

Stockton's decision to comply with David's request caused us to bypass a significant part of our pre-dive process that was designed to ensure crew safety. We were introducing a huge amount of risk. I pulled Stockton aside and shared my concerns.

"Relax," he said. "It's not going to be a problem."

"Famous last words. Look, you're probably right, but can we walk through the risk analysis anyway?"

"Okay. First, we can both agree that David is not the risk, right?

I mean, the guy has done so much more than what we're doing today. This is going to be a walk in the park for him."

"Maybe, but he's like six-foot-four. He says he's not claustrophobic, but how often has he squeezed himself into a space as small as *Antipodes*? I'm sure he'll be fine, but you have to admit that's a risk."

"Yeah, but, what, like a 2 percent chance that he freaks out? I can live with that."

"Fine. You're probably right. What about his girlfriend?"

"Okay, she's probably the real risk, but we're going to have to defer to David on this. I spoke with him on the phone and explained everything we'll be doing. He assured me she'd be fine. He's not going to want to put her at risk, so he said he spoke with her about it and walked her through it. She's excited about it. I'm sure she'll be fine, too. Besides, I'll be the pilot, so I'll assess her from the moment they arrive at the marina."

"Neither of them are going to be familiar with our operations, especially the crew transfers. You know that's usually the riskiest part of the mission."

"That's why I'm going to drive the boat out to the dive site myself. I'll have all that time to brief them."

"I guess that would work."

"Look, you're in charge. If you want to cancel it, just let me know and I'll call David. I'm sure he'll understand."

"No! I want to do this as much as you do. If anything, I'm curious to see how an experienced explorer handles his first dive in our sub. I just want to make sure we have everything covered, so it all goes smoothly, even if something goes sideways."

"The weather and sea conditions are cooperating, right?"

"Yup."

"Then we should be fine," said Stockton. "Yes, we're taking on additional risk, but how much risk, really? Given David's experience, probably not that much. And the reward could be huge, if we want to get him on our board. At a minimum, hopefully we'll have a lifelong advocate for our cause."

"I know the risk-reward analysis is fine. I just want to make sure you and I are on the same page."

"Done."

"Just to be safe, I'm going to be the one waiting on the deck of the sub for you when you arrive."

"I wouldn't want it any other way."

"Between the two of us and the dinghy driver, we'll make sure the crew transfers go well."

"Sounds good."

Later that day, the entire dive operation went off without a hitch. Our team pre-positioned the sub at the dive site before David and his girlfriend arrived and then returned it to the marina after they departed. Stockton drove them in the boat to and from the dive site. We transferred them on and off *Antipodes* without any issues. And, of course, they had an amazing two-hour dive exploring the deep canyons off the coast of Monterey. David and his girlfriend had smiles on their faces when they left, and David ultimately served on OceanGate's board of directors for one term.

The team had not been comfortable with our last-minute decision to "cut corners," but ultimately they had deferred to me and Stockton and our risk-reward analysis. We were fortunate that the weather held up and the sea conditions were particularly mild. We were also lucky that nothing major went wrong with the sub, the dinghy, the support boat, or the speed boat, as often seems to happen with all sub operations. Then again, if anything unexpected *had* come up, our normal safety protocols would have kicked in, regardless of any other risk-reward analysis. I would have made sure of that, and Stockton would have, too.

He and I would often talk about risk, and we were always on the same page. Neither of us was a risk-taker. We each considered ourselves risk managers. In order to manage risks, we had to first understand the potential risks, identify actual risks, and assess the probability of each risk as well as the result of each risk. Then we had to do the same for the rewards that followed those risks, since they were the twin pillars of a risk-reward analysis. We always said that some people just had a higher tolerance for where those analysis results landed on the risk spectrum.

Coming from our space backgrounds, we always found it ridiculous that people considered us "risk takers" or "risk lovers" without ever doing any risk-reward analysis in their own lives. After all, most people ignore the fact that statistically some of the riskiest activities they can take on are crossing the street, driving a car, and staying home (since most people die in their own homes). The fact is that people who engage in what others see as risky activities (such as sub diving, flying airplanes, exploration, skydiving, bungee jumping, rock climbing, and so on) are usually just "risk managers" who happen to have a high tolerance for risk, mostly because they understand the risks they are taking on.

As Stockton used to say, "If you're an explorer, then risk is just a part of your life you have to embrace, so you might as well be proactive about managing it."

Winter 2012
Miami, Florida

IT WAS STILL DARK WHEN WE PULLED OUT OF THE MARINA. THE WEATHER looked good, and we got off on time, so we would be heading out with the ebbing tide. The sun would come up soon, but by then, we should have been past the breakwater and onto the open ocean. It was frosty that morning, something we thought we were leaving behind when we relocated the sub from Seattle to South Florida.

Stockton was slotted as the pilot for that day's dive, and I would be topside as Mission Director, so we had some time to kill while the rest of the crew took us out to the dive site. We both preferred early mornings, when we could catch up during the tow. As we got underway, the pilot on comms for that day used her cell phone to call the Coast Guard's Watch Commander to let them know we were heading out. We had already pre-filed our dive plan, so the call went smoothly, as usual. She entered the call in the log.

"How's it been with this sector? All good?" Stockton asked.

"Yeah, for the most part," I replied. "It was rough at first, since they had some turnover at the sector command. Plus they're a little skittish around here, given how much strange shit they see.

But I think it actually helped that the DEA and Border Patrol were interested in us. They're so nervous about the cartels using subs to smuggle drugs into US waters that I think they see us as an extra set of eyes and ears out there."

"How the hell would that work? It's not like we'll just randomly have our sub stumble across a cartel sub running along the bottom of the ocean."

"I have no idea, but I don't care. As long as it keeps us on their good side."

"So what's the process here? The same as Seattle?"

"Pretty much," I replied. "They haven't sent anyone out to inspect us, but they accept our dive plans and appreciate when we call them on the way out and back. Apparently, they get radio calls from other boaters when they see our sub, thinking we're a drug sub."

"Remember the shit-show in LA? Or Long Beach? Or wherever that was? What a nightmare!"

"Yeah, well, I think we just got spoiled in Seattle. What was that Chief Warrant Officer's name? Winters? He was awesome. He really set us up and helped get his commander on board."

"He wasn't awesome so much as he was reasonable and had common sense," said Stockton. "He actually took the time to educate himself on the regs and our operation."

"And he appreciated that we were making an effort to comply with regs that even he admitted were crap. Remember when he even went on our cert dive?"

"Oh, yeah. How'd he end up on that dive again?"

"We scheduled the ABS surveyor to come out for the 1,000-foot dive, and then at the last minute, he said that his girlfriend wouldn't let him dive in the sub."

"She wouldn't let him do his job. She probably should've thought about that before they started dating."

"Yup. It was ridiculous. Thank God the surveyor was willing to accept a Coast Guard rep as his proxy and that Winters was willing and available to jump in as a last-minute replacement. And we had fun poking around along the bottom until you found the one spot in Puget Sound that got us to 1,000 feet. I think Winters was even more excited than we were."

"Yeah, that was a fun dive. Great guy."

"And the San Francisco sector was pretty good, too," I recalled. "They were really cool with our ops in Monterey, and I think they were actually disappointed that we canceled Alcatraz. They even tried helping us convince HQ to make some changes to the regs."

"Too bad that never went anywhere."

"Well, you gotta appreciate the HQ guy's position. There just aren't enough subs to justify the Coast Guard's use of taxpayer funds to update the regs, especially if they have to get congressional approval. As that guy told us, he's tasked with public safety, not economic development."

"The American taxpayer in me agrees, but it's still frustrating, because then we get that jerk in LA."

"Yeah, I still don't know what his problem was. I mean, I understand that he's got a huge-ass sector to cover and that Long Beach is one of the busiest ports in the country, but all he wanted to do was say no. He wouldn't even try to see our perspective. He was just itching to send boats out to shut us down. At least now we can scratch one sector off our list. We're never going back there again."

"At some point, we're going to have to explore a couple of other sectors."

"Or we can take our show on the road and get the heck out of the US. This is painful. It's got to be easier in other countries."

"Maybe. It can't possibly get any worse."

"Or can it?"

Summer 2012

Miami, Florida

"WHAT IS THE COOLEST THING YOU'VE EVER SEEN DOWN THERE?" THIS IS by far the most common question every sub pilot gets.

I have my own personal answer, but for Stockton's, I had the privilege of experiencing a dive that was the epitome of our founding vision, even though I was on the support ship when it happened and not in the sub itself. It was also one of my favorite memories of Stockton.

We had planned a mission to explore a few unknown sonar targets about five miles off the coast of Miami. Stockton was in town, as was Chris Welsh, the adventurer who had purchased Graham's *DeepFlight Challenger* from Steve Fossett's estate. We decided that the two of them would come out to pilot one of our dives, taking with them three of our other team members. I would act as Mission Director on the support boat, joined by a boat captain, a communications officer, and a deck hand.

The dive started innocently enough. They were operating at about 250 feet (75 meters). From the surface, we guided them to the first sonar target. A cement block. Boring. They reached the second target. A sailboat. Interesting, but not uncommon. We gave them distance and bearing to the third target.

They were delayed calling up in the time we estimated they would arrive there. Just as we were starting to worry, Chris keyed the sub's microphone and started transmitting from below. However, none of us on the boat could hear him because the other four people in the sub were all talking loudly, clearly excited about something. When we asked him to repeat his transmission, again we could not make out exactly what he was saying.

After the second transmission, I looked at the boat captain and asked, "Did I hear one of them say 'airplane'?" He nodded, as confused as I was. The comms officer asked for clarification, and Chris confirmed.

The third target was an airplane!

When we finally got them all back on the boat, they could not stop talking, smiling, and high-fiving. They showed us photos and videos of their discovery. It was a World War II fighter plane! It was incredibly intact, lying upside down on the ocean floor. Clearly it had been ditched by the pilot, likely in the early 1940s.

We were all fairly certain that no commercial diver or submersible had ever been there, so I looked at Stockton and said, "Do you realize that the last human to see that plane was probably the pilot seventy years ago? And you five are the first ones to see it underwater? Now *that* is exploration!"

I will never forget the excitement on Stockton's face from that dive. This was precisely the personal passion that had driven him to start OceanGate. This made all of the sacrifices worthwhile.

In an interesting postscript to this story, we later contacted the US Navy to inquire about the plane, and they confirmed it was a Grumman F6F Hellcat that had experienced an engine failure shortly after takeoff, forcing the pilot to bail out into the ocean. He survived, but the plane sank. That was 1941.

They sent one of their historians out to confirm the find, and a crew from CBS News documented the whole mission. Not only did we end up on national news, but also our footage of the wreck ran on one of the big screens in New York's Time Square for quite some time.

It was our first brush with fame as a company, and it felt like confirmation that we were heading in the right direction.

Chapter 9

LION'S DEN

November 2023

New Orleans, Louisiana

We poured out of the Uber and started walking toward the convention center. I stopped, turned around, and asked the four guys to gather around me for a minute. I felt like I needed to say something before we went in.

"I just want to thank you guys for being here with me for this," I stammered. "I'm not sure what to expect these next couple of days, but I'm sure I couldn't make it through without your support."

I grew unexpectedly emotional and could barely finish my thoughts. They understood, patted me on the back, and together we turned to go inside.

We were in New Orleans for the annual three-day Submarine Symposium event (formerly held in conjunction with Underwater Intervention, or UI), the only time every year that the entire global submersible community—designers, builders, operators, and agencies—gathered in one place. It was going to be the first event since the June accident, and I felt a moral obligation to attend, in my mind perhaps as a tribute to Stockton.

My four friends were a team of independent filmmakers that I had decided to help develop a documentary telling the story of Stockton, OceanGate, *Titan*, and the accident. The lead producer and I had been friends for fifteen years, and he had met Stockton and dived with him in *Antipodes*. He had been impacted by the shock of the incident, and this documentary was his way of coping with the loss.

I had last attended UI over a decade prior while I was still with OceanGate and an active participant in the community. At the time, the event had been organized by the Marine Technology Society (MTS) Manned Underwater Vessel Committee, and I had once been chair of the MTS Ocean Exploration Committee. In a way, I was coming home.

However, it was a home that had changed dramatically during my absence.

Most importantly, over the years the members and senior leaders of the group had become increasingly concerned with the approach Stockton and OceanGate were taking in the development of the *Titan* submersible, and so they had distanced themselves from the whole effort. In the media frenzy that June, many of the most vocal members of the community had also been vocal in the mass media. In 2018, this group of industry experts had drafted and signed a letter to Stockton imploring him to stop his development program for fear of catastrophic results due to his purported poor design and testing methods. Five years later, this letter gained public notoriety through the global media attention following the accident.

In a very real way, rather than coming home, I felt like I was walking into a lion's den.

Over the next few days I would be reunited with people like Patrick Lahey, Will Kohnen, Karl Stanley, and many others whose names had gained public attention in the mass media for rebuking Stockton and blaming him for a tragedy they felt could have been avoided. I kept telling myself that it would be alright and that they would be duly respectful, professional, and considerate. After all, I had always had a collegial working relationship with each of them, and I had left the company before the start of the *Titan* development program that they so reviled. Their beef was with Stockton, not with me.

Nevertheless, my stomach was doing cartwheels as we made our way up the escalators to the area where the talks and meetings would take place. My brain was in a fog, and I felt numb when we finally arrived.

It turned out that I was right. Everyone welcomed me back into the fold and was happy to speak with me. As I expected, they were all respectful, professional, and considerate—at least in their direct interactions with me.

However, as I sat through the first few presentations, it was clear that the OceanGate accident had cast a pall on the proceedings in a way no one had ever experienced.

In his welcoming remarks to open the talks, Will, the organizer, paid tribute to two legends who had passed away since the last event, Phil Nuytten and Don Walsh. He then moved on to review the agenda for our event, and my phone buzzed.

"No mention of Stockton?!" texted my friend the producer, who was sitting at the other end of the room.

I had also noticed that glaring omission.

Then again, Phil Nuytten had been a submersible designer, pilot, and community ambassador for more than four decades. Likewise, Don Walsh was not only one of the first two human beings to reach the deepest point in the ocean back in 1960, but he had also remained a global icon for ocean exploration for over six decades. Even Stockton would not have dared to consider himself on par with those two legends.

Still, Will sent a clear message by not even acknowledging the loss of the five *Titan* crew members in his opening eulogy.

A few minutes later, I started to discover why.

The rest of the first day's program consisted of talks on familiar topics about the status of the global submersible community, announcements about new sub designs, and discussions about various topics related to submersible operations, safety, and regulations. Sadly, these familiar topics were tainted by recent events, and every speaker made sure to mention the *Titan* tragedy, usually as an example of what *not* to do. There was also at least one talk that was clearly new, since it was a detailed review of the search and rescue operations for the *Titan* crew.

Throughout the day, I occasionally pulled people aside to have a conversation with me for the documentary. A sound engineer would put microphones on us, and the director would capture us on camera. Perhaps not surprisingly, everyone was amenable to being recorded and engaged in measured discussions with me, but they definitely did not hold back when it came to their ongoing criticism of Stockton. They certainly disagreed with his design and testing methodologies, but they were especially stung by his disdain for the community's well-established best practices for safety.

As the day drew to a close, I reflected on what I had heard, seen, and experienced. I jotted down some notes. Over the next couple of days, my initial thoughts were confirmed.

Mostly, I was struck by the hypocrisy of the community members and their inability to acknowledge it. In very public statements to the media in the immediate aftermath of the accident, they had skewered Stockton for various deviations from what they considered the proper way to design, build, and operate submersibles in a safe manner. However, during the conference they were unknowingly (or perhaps knowingly) admitting to each other that they were doing many of the same things.

For example, one of the main public critiques was their assertion that the only safe material for building deep submersibles was titanium. They could not believe that Stockton would push ahead with using carbon fiber for the pressure hull, when clearly titanium was the only way to go. I could understand that argument, since every deep-diving submersible before *Titan* had been made out of titanium. However, one of the event presenters used his time onstage to effusively announce his company's new deep-diving submersible that would be made out of acrylic and another that would be made out of glass. I could not believe my ears. I felt like shouting, "I love that you're innovating with new materials, but why did you have to go on record to lambaste Stockton for not using titanium if you're also not using titanium?"

Likewise, another public critique was based on *Titan*'s cylindrical hull. According to industry experts, the only acceptable form factor to withstand the intense pressures of the deep ocean was a sphere. However, another presenter proudly announced a new design that was shaped like an "ovaloid" and affectionately called it their "Tic Tac Sub." Again, I was impressed by his company's innovation and truly supported it, but I just could not understand how that same person could have been on camera with a journalist just a few months prior knocking down *Titan* for not being a sphere.

And yet the biggest hypocrisy was on the question of classing a new sub.

During the event, I had several conversations with representatives from various sub builders, as well as the lead from one of the two classing agencies. It was clear from their responses to my questions that there was no way OceanGate could have gotten *Titan* classed, not so much because the sub was not safe but more because at the time, neither of the classing societies was equipped to process such a radical new design concept.

Apparently, the leading classing group now has over a dozen engineers working in its submersible division, but they had none when *Titan* was going through development. This is how some of the current innovative sub designs are successfully securing classification, which is certainly a positive step in the right direction for humanity. However, it is also precisely why I believe Stockton chose not to pursue classification several years ago. A couple of industry insiders even admitted to me privately that Stockton may have been ahead of his time and that things would be much different if he was starting the *Titan* development program today.

Besides the hypocrisy, I was also reminded of how small the

global sub community really is. The media kept calling this an "industry," but it is difficult to categorize anything as such when there are only four major sub builders in the world (all of them primarily for recreational use) and only a few dozen subs in operation. During one of the opening talks, the speaker gave a numerical update on the state of the community, and he noted that there were only 190 subs in the world. Of those, only thirteen were capable of diving beyond 1,000 meters (about 3,300 feet) (as a reminder, *Titan* was rated to 4,000 meters [about 13,000 feet]). During a different presentation, I was able to confirm with the speaker—a representative from the US Coast Guard—that there are currently only three subs operating in US waters, and they are all tourist subs taking passengers to only 30 meters (about 100 feet) operated by Atlantis Submarines in Hawaii.

Despite my ten-year absence, sadly this was still very much only a global community and not a true industry.

I left New Orleans with mixed feelings.

On the one hand, I was happy to see the immense progress that the community was making in technology innovation and expanding humanity's access to the deep oceans. After all, this was the core motivation behind our founding of OceanGate. For better or worse, I felt proud that in one way or another we—and especially Stockton—had played a pivotal role in that evolution and growth.

On the other hand, I was sad to know that Stockton was not around to witness this progress in person. I was even more upset that the key individuals leading this community not only refused to recognize his contributions but even held him in contempt as a counterexample of a "proper" approach to innovation.

Perhaps they are right. Or not. I imagine that, as with other visionaries, Stockton's legacy will ultimately be cast only by the passage of time.

Chapter 10

CLASSING NEW SUBS AND *TITANIC*

Fall 2012

Miami, Florida

STOCKTON AND I STOOD IN THE PARKING LOT ON THE MIAMI RIVER. Below us, our team was conducting yet another dockside test of the LRT system, with *Antipodes* still secured by a crane, just in case anything went wrong. Always safety first. It was a busy time for OceanGate since we had just purchased our second sub from an operator in the Azores, and we would soon be transitioning into the next phase of our growth plan. There would be many changes coming in the next few weeks and months.

Earlier in the year, we had already split our team geographically. Some of our core team and the fledgling engineering group had stayed in Seattle with Stockton, while I brought the sub and the ops team to Miami, where we also hired a few new people. Then we had decided to go ahead with the next step in our succession plan by making Stockton the CEO and moving me into the COO role. These were two huge changes for a small company like OceanGate, but they were necessary to prepare us for the bigger changes on the way.

We needed to transition from our core business focus as a sub operator to a greater focus as a sub designer and builder. For the next few years, the work of the engineering team would take priority over the work of the ops team. Seattle would become more important than Miami, and Stockton would play a greater role than I would. Again, Stockton and I had planned all of this and agreed to it. We were fully committed to our founding vision and to the plan that we were convinced would get us there. Now it was merely a matter of executing that plan.

Stockton had become increasingly convinced that our deep 6,000-meter subs would have pressure hulls made out of carbon fiber, mostly to keep the weight down in order to make them easily transportable. He had spent a couple of years conducting extensive research, developing different designs, and building computer models for testing. We knew that getting something that innovative from concept to operations would be a tremendous undertaking that would require time, resources, and capital. I trusted Stockton to get us through the R&D process successfully, and I was confident that we could pull it off. The only question was how much time we would need.

Of course, despite our optimism, we recognized that there was significant risk in our plan. Not safety risk, because our ops team had already honed our safety protocols in our dive operations.

Rather, technology risk. We were still not sure if carbon fiber would actually work for a deep sub, and, even if it did, we were not sure how long it would take us to get such a sub into full operation.

In order to manage this business risk, Stockton came up with a "parallel path" approach.

The engineering team would need time to get the carbon fiber hull through all of the design and testing processes, and this would likely take a few years. In the meantime, we wanted to develop and test all of the other systems for the new sub, including power, life support, navigation, communications, and so on. We figured that those could be configured independently from the carbon fiber hull and did not even need to be taken as deep. All we needed was a standard titanium pressure hull to use as a "technology test bed" for these new systems.

We thought about commissioning a new titanium pressure hull from a certified experienced builder, but we could not justify the cost and time for something that we saw as quite temporary and only a means to an end. We carefully considered using *Antipodes* for this purpose, but ultimately we decided that we liked having a fully functional nonexperimental sub for any mission opportunities that might come our way. Instead, we went back into the market to look for another used sub that might be for sale. Actually, the sub itself did not matter too much for our purposes, since all we really wanted was the pressure hull.

When we found the *Lula 500* in the Azores, we knew our search was over.

This was a two-person sub capable of diving to 500 meters (1,650 feet) in a cylindrical titanium hull that would be perfect for us. We hired Pete Hoffmann to help us negotiate the purchase, and then he and I went to the Azores for the final inspection. The sub was now on its way to Florida, after which we planned to drive it on a flatbed truck across the country to Seattle. The engineering team would then strip it down to the hull and refit it with all of the new systems that were being designed for our future deep subs. We did not know it at the time, but this process would end up taking two years, and the new sub would be named *Cyclops*.

"So, are you excited to get your hands on *Lula* and finally get the party started?" I asked.

"Yeah, there's a lot to do," Stockton replied.

"No kidding! At least we'll have time. We've got the funding in place, we've got *Antipodes* for any ops, and you've got a plan for the carbon fiber. Other than hiring a few folks and bringing on some strategic partners, it should just be a matter of executing, right?"

"I just want to get diving already. *Antipodes* is nice, but it's just our training wheels sub. We need to get deep. Even *Lula* won't help with that."

"We'll get there!"

"Not soon enough."

"Hey, shifting gears a little, what's your current thinking on classing *Lula*? Its ABS certificate is still valid, so we'd only need to do an annual survey."

"Why would we go through the trouble of classing a sub that we're going to dismantle? That seems like a total waste of time and money."

"What about when the refit is done? If we want that sub classed, we might want to keep ABS in the loop even before we start the process."

"Nah, we can bring them in after we finish the refit. If we even want to class the new sub," Stockton added.

"Wait. What? Are you thinking that we might not want to have this one classed?"

"Well, you know how I feel about the whole classing system. It's just a con scheme for ABS and Lloyd's to make money. They don't add any value. They don't provide any real engineering peer review, especially on new innovations that aren't part of the current standards. They don't provide any safety coverage because that would expose them to ridiculous legal liability. And for our business, I'm not convinced we even need the certificate. I mean, how many times have we been asked for *Antipodes*' certificate? Zero. Even when we try using it as a selling point for charter customers, no one knows what it means to be an 'ABS-classed sub.' It's just a waste of time and money. I'd rather avoid it completely."

"I know. We've talked about that a million times. But *Lula* is already classed, so isn't there value in keeping that certificate active? Just like with *Antipodes*?"

"Maybe. Then again, at this point, we have no idea how many changes we're going to make on the systems for that hull. Knowing how ABS operates, I'll bet that they won't consider this a simple refit and just rubber-stamp our renewal. They'll see an opportunity to make more money by calling it a 'new design' or a 'new sub,' just so they can charge us more fees."

"Well, in that case, I'd agree with you that it'd be a waste of time and money. We're probably not going to be operating that sub any more than *Antipodes*, since it's just part of the R&D process. We're more focused on the deep subs anyway."

"Exactly."

"Speaking of the deep subs," I continued, "do you think we'll ever get those classed? I know that you don't want to feed their con game, but at least those subs will be our ultimate 'product' that we'll be presenting to the world. They won't be like *Antipodes,* the training wheels sub, or *Lula,* the tech testbed sub. They'll be our 'fully operational fleet of innovative carbon fiber deep-diving' subs. They'll be the first of their kind. For those, people may want to feel comfortable that some third-party gave them a thumbs-up."

"Maybe. But there are other ways to inspire confidence without giving in to the class society con game. I think the best way is to have a solid ops track record. If we just dive those subs over and over without any incidents, then people won't even question the engineering or design."

"Agreed. And while we're doing those dives to build up that track record, we can just designate them as 'experimental subs,' just like Graham did with his winged subs."

"Which also has the benefit of being true, since we'll still be experimenting with them for a long time," Stockton pointed out. "Besides, you and I both know that neither of the classing societies knows anything about carbon fiber. We'd have to teach them everything we know just to get them to the point where they feel comfortable signing off on a certificate. They don't have any standards for using carbon fiber in deep subs, so we're basically going to have to write the standards for them, just like the Atlantis guys did for the Coast Guard on their tourist subs. The difference is that the Coast Guard didn't charge Atlantis to develop those regs, but you know that ABS is going to charge us a shit-ton of fees for the privilege of educating them and writing their standards for them. It's such a sleazy business."

"Just like insurance, where they make money by convincing you to bet against yourself."

"Exactly. Like I've told you before about insurance, sometimes I think that we should start our own classing society. It'd be a total money-making venture. Then again, I'd feel too slimy to do it, so never mind."

"Also, I never understood how new innovations can become industry standards without giving the industry enough time to try different approaches."

"Yeah, that too. I mean, I've run a ton of computer models already, but we're going to have to run so many more before we even start building any of the hulls. Then we're going to go through several hulls in lab testing before we even start diving. Then we're going to go dive several hulls before we can finally feel like we're settled on a design. During that whole time, we'll be an experimental sub, because it just doesn't make any sense to even try getting it classed with the design in constant flux. However, even once we've settled on our final design, it still won't make sense to get it classed even if we wanted to, because how can one company's design be considered the industry standard when there won't be any other competing designs to choose from?"

"You mean with carbon fiber hulls."

"Right. There will be other deep-diving sub designs with titanium hulls, but we'll be the only ones operating with carbon fiber hulls. Would humanity really be served well if the entire world had to comply with OceanGate's standard for carbon fiber hulls? Hell no!"

"But you agree that safety standards are important, right?" I asked. "I mean, we have them for cars, airplanes, ships, and lots of other things."

"Of course, but look at how those standards are developed. First, those are developed by government agencies, not by private organizations. That's one huge difference. If public safety is really the priority, then public funds should be used to oversee it. In the sub world, these are not publicly funded government agencies, but private ventures that rely on charging fees to the very people they are supposed to be reviewing. That seems like a huge conflict of interest to me."

"Of course it is," I agreed.

"Second, in those other industries, safety standards are developed over long periods of time where agencies have lots of different data points to draw from. Right now, there are strict safety standards for seat belts in cars, but that's because there have been many different companies making millions of seat belts trying different designs. Whatever agency sets those seat belt standards can review the data on all of the different designs and pick the best practices to set as an industry standard. Our sub community just isn't nearly big enough to develop anything close to what any reasonable person could consider an industry standard."

"There are some basic things."

"Yeah, sure, we can all agree that titanium is a good material for deep subs, but that's just because it's what humanity has used for a century. You're telling me that we have to ignore all of the advances in material sciences just because titanium has been proven to work? What about carbon fiber? What about acrylic? What about glass? There are a ton of other materials we could use, but guess what, none of them are considered industry standards. At least not for deep subs."

"And there's the safety angle, right?"

"Right. That's the most hypocritical part of the whole thing that drives me crazy. Justifying the fees they're going to charge by playing the 'safety' card. That's disgusting. Just because titanium was the best we could come up with a century ago and just because it has a proven track record doesn't mean that it's necessarily the safest material to use. Is it safe? Sure. Can the industry do better? I'm sure we can. Given the pace of engineering innovation, I'd be shocked if we couldn't. More importantly, shouldn't we be actively promoting sub designers to come up with better, safer designs?"

"I still can't believe that we're having to do this on our own. Why can't the Triton or SEAmagine guys see this? I mean, they already have some of the best sub engineers in the world. They're smart guys, and they've got innovative ideas. I know they've got their own business models that rely on selling subs that are classed, but c'mon."

"Well, like you said, they've got their business models. They use that class certificate as part of their sales pitch, and it works for their customers. So they just bake the time and money of the certification process into the cost of the sub, and their customers pay for it. In a way, they just become an extension of the classing society con game. They're just helping them con the ultimate customers who buy the subs from them."

"To be fair, it's not really 'conning the sub buyers,' because the subs are, in fact, classed. Maybe it's more like just overstating the importance of that certificate during the sales pitch."

"To-may-to, to-mah-to."

"Stockton, I know we've said this before many times, but remind me again, why did we get ourselves into this crazy business?"

"Beats me. Sometimes I think Elon had it easier trying to send rockets to space."

"I'm sure he'd disagree."

"Only because he hasn't tried building a sub business!" Stockton exclaimed.

Fall 2012

Miami, Florida

I CALLED IT "BLUE PLANET EXPEDITIONS." I SAW IT AS THE ONLY WAY I could possibly continue adding value to OceanGate now that Stockton was CEO. We were moving quickly into the next phase of our strategic plan, and pretty soon the primary focus of the company would be the engineering effort that he would be leading in Seattle. If I was going to stay with OceanGate, as Stockton kept confirming he wanted, then I had to find a viable path forward. He tasked me with whiteboarding my ideal role over the next five years, and this is what I had come up with.

I started with a bit of self-reflection to determine what made me happy. Since we started OceanGate, I felt most at home during our expeditions. That was where I could leverage all of my leadership skills and where I thought I was most helpful to the company. Also, it was where I felt most connected to the personal passion that had driven both of us to the submersible world in the first place: exploration.

I wanted to organize and lead many more ocean exploration expeditions using our submersibles, continuing with *Antipodes* and ultimately culminating with our future fleet of deep subs. I imagined our ops team working with scientists and filmmakers to make groundbreaking discoveries and to create inspirational stories. This was how I wanted to spend the next five—or even twenty-five—years of my life.

However, OceanGate was not an ocean exploration business. We had specifically set up the company as a sub charter business. Our model was to generate revenue by charging ocean exploration expeditions for the use of our subs, not to conduct the expeditions ourselves. I realized that the vision I had painted for myself was not really to work at OceanGate but rather to work at one of OceanGate's customers.

That revelation disheartened me, but then I came up with what I thought was a creative way to reconcile the discrepancy.

In order to convince prospective expedition customers to charter our subs, we would have to demonstrate our subs' capabilities as well as our team's proficiency. We believed that eventually we would have enough of a proven track record that we could simply rely on case studies, testimonials, and referrals. Until then, we would have to invest in marketing.

And that was the source of my idea for Blue Planet Expeditions.

Originally conceived as a marketing program for OceanGate, it would consist of a series of exploration expeditions to showcase our subs and our ops team. We would start with the first descent of a crewed submersible into one of the world's deepest underwater caverns, Dean's Blue Hole in the Bahamas. This would be followed by an expedition into the shallower but much more popular Belize Blue Hole. That would probably take us a couple of years, by which time our refitted *Lula* sub would be available and we could get creative with slightly deeper targets or with diving both subs together. By the time our deep subs came online, we would have a strong track record of expeditions and a full pipeline of charter customers, so we could use our Blue Planet Expeditions marketing program mostly to highlight the capabilities of the new deep subs by picking targets that were previously unattainable to us with our shallower subs.

Every expedition would have a core group of scientists specifically recruited for the mission objectives, as well as a professional film production team to document the entire effort. It would be pure exploration for the purpose of scientific discovery and inspirational storytelling.

I knew Stockton would love it, but I also knew it would never work inside OceanGate. I had to give it a shot anyway.

"So, whaddya think?" I asked, after he finished reading my proposal.

"You already know what I think."

"You love it, but not for OceanGate."

"Exactly. You estimated $1 million over the next two years for these first blue hole expeditions. You know we can't afford that out of our marketing budget. Not even close."

"Well, I put in there that we might be able to subsidize this through some brand sponsorships. That's how David de Rothschild funded all of his expeditions. In fact, remember him telling us that he felt they had left money on the table? Maybe we could even turn this into a profit center for us."

"Then we'd have to invest in a sponsorship sales team, right? He also told us that corporate marketing departments have long sales cycles for their sponsorships, so it might even take us a couple of years to close most of those deals. And he also told us the chicken-and-egg problem he faced with his early expeditions. Brands don't want to invest in an expedition unless they're sure it's going to happen, but you can't be sure an expedition is going to happen unless sponsors sign up. I just don't see how we get there," Stockton said.

"How about if we raise the money from investors? We could give them a share of the sponsorship revenues and film royalties."

"Maybe, but we just did a raise, and we pitched them on our engineering focus. I don't want to go out again, especially now with a totally different pitch. We'll sound completely schizophrenic."

"I know, I know."

"What about offering this to Mission Specialists? We really haven't pushed this idea much so far, mostly because it's just a way to comply with the Coast Guard regs here in US waters, but what about creating a full package."

"Like the Deep Ocean Expeditions guys?" I asked.

"Something like that," he said. "I mean DOE is charging people $25K, $30K, even $60K just for a visit to the *Titanic* in those spartan *Mir* subs from the Russians. We could probably charge something similar for these expeditions you sketched out."

"But then we'd be a tourism company. First, that wouldn't fit inside OceanGate. Second, that's the antithesis of why you and I got into subs to begin with. We want to explore, not carry passengers on sightseeing tours."

"You're right that it can't be OceanGate, but maybe we could spin out a wholly owned subsidiary as a separate business?" he suggested.

"That seems like a complete distraction. I'm pretty sure our investors would cringe if they found out any amount of their funds was being used for that effort."

"That's why the spin-out might work. We could raise money from different investors into that subsidiary."

"Who's going to do that raise?" I asked. "You can't be distracted by it."

"Well, you could become CEO of the subsidiary. Then you could do the raise."

"Stockton, there's no way I'm going to run a tourism business, and I'm certainly not going to raise money from investors for a tourism business. Even if I wanted to, I'm not the right guy for that job."

"So we recruit someone who is."

"Ugh! It really doesn't seem worth the effort. Or risk. Plus, even if we're successful, then all we'll have is a tourism business, which neither of us has ever been interested in."

"Hey, I didn't say I liked my idea. I'm just trying to salvage your idea."

"Yeah, I get that. Thanks," I said. "But even if we wanted to go through all of this effort and even if we were successful in raising the money for this new tourism business, this idea still wouldn't work. At least not the way I originally envisioned it. Most of the expeditions I scoped out are for exploration. We'll be going places no one has been before. We can't take untrained civilians. That's way too much risk from a safety standpoint and from a mission accomplishment standpoint. These expeditions need to be limited to the ops team, the science team, and the production team. Professionals only."

"Agreed. So change the expeditions. Instead of going places no one has been before, we go to places people have been before. Places that are more known and understood. For example, we scratch Dean's Blue Hole, since no one has dived there before, but we keep the Belize Blue Hole, since even scuba divers go there all the time."

I considered this. "So you mean change the objectives from exploration to sightseeing?"

"Not exactly," said Stockton. "We could still keep the science and storytelling objectives, since that would fit nicely with the Mission Specialist concept. We just need to change our target selection criteria."

"Maybe. I guess that keeping the citizen science element could still make it interesting for us, even if we're stuck going places people have been before."

"And eventually, we'll get charter customers who want our subs for exploration expeditions, so we'll still get to explore. It'll just be paid by someone else."

"Okay, I could see this working. I'm still not sure that it's something I want to spend the next five years of my life working on, but I could see it fitting in with OceanGate. Especially if we can set it up as a subsidiary with someone else running it and raising money from other investors."

"Here's another benefit for OceanGate: The subsidiary could even charter the subs from the parent company, so these expeditions would look like customer revenue to us."

"That's true. And totally legit," I added. "From OceanGate's perspective, the subsidiary's expeditions look just like a charter customer. Even if we give them a steep discount as a sister company, that's still revenue on our P&L. Plus, we could use them as case studies in our marketing materials, especially if the subsidiary is branded differently. Like, say, Blue Planet Expeditions?"

"Even if it was called OceanGate Expeditions, it's still perfectly reasonable customer revenue. To your point, it still helps us showcase the subs and the ops team."

"Wait. Now I'm thinking ahead. For *Antipodes* and for the *Lula* refit, I'm sure we can find nonexploration targets since those are relatively shallow subs. There are thousands of shipwrecks, reefs, and other destinations that are well-known and well-documented but still have scientific value. But we won't have that for the deep subs. I mean, the whole reason our founding vision was for 6,000-meter subs was precisely to help humanity fill in our massive knowledge gap of the deep ocean. There just aren't that many targets we could identify for these 'science-but-not-exploration' expeditions."

"Well, you know my favorite," said Stockton.

"Hydrothermal vents?"

"Yup."

"Yeah, but even those are still exploration. That's why you're so excited about them, right? Same with the deep corals that NOAA wants us to explore."

"Hmmm. Well, if we want something deep that has already been explored, then there's really only one potential target I can think of."

"*Titanic*?" I asked.

"Exactly. DOE is already going there with the *Mir* subs, so maybe we could do the same?"

"Ugh! I have absolutely zero interest in going to the *Titanic*, let alone doing it to take paying passengers who want to serve as Mission Specialists."

"Me neither," he said. "I still can't understand the fanatical interest that so many people have in that wreck. I've never wanted to go there. I don't understand why Cameron is so fixated on it."

"Well, regardless, since DOE is already going there, wouldn't it be easier to simply sell them a charter on our deep subs, whenever they're ready? This could give them an alternative to the *Mir*s. We could talk with Rob McCallum about this." Rob was one of the most experienced expedition leaders in the world, and he had been heading up DOE's expeditions to the *Titanic*.

"You're right. It would be easier. And more effective. After all, they're already set up as a tourism business that organizes *Titanic* trips, so why compete with them? We can just get them as a charter customer."

"Assuming they're still in business by the time our deep subs are ready," I said. "Didn't they just cancel their centennial expedition because the Russians pulled the plug on the two subs? If they can't get them to restart the *Mir* program, then DOE's going to be screwed. None of the other government subs capable of reaching *Titanic* will ever agree to a commercial charter contract. Do you think DOE can wait two or three years until our deep subs are ready?"

"We can always talk with them about it. Maybe we chase them as our primary plan but we use our subsidiary as a backup plan? We can still go forward with your Blue Planet Expeditions plan using *Antipodes* and then the new *Lula* refit. Then we can revisit everything as the deep subs get closer to coming online."

"So the plan would be for me to create a wholly owned subsidiary, recruit a CEO, and help the CEO raise money for a science-based ocean tourism business that uses OceanGate's subs on a charter basis. Did I summarize that right?"

Stockton nodded. "Yeah, I think so."

"I don't know. I'd have to think about it. It's not really what I want to do. It seems like a very long convoluted road to get somewhere that isn't even what I was originally envisioning. I don't know if I'll be happy spending my time doing this."

"And if it's not worth your time, then it certainly isn't worth mine. I have to focus on building our new subs."

"Right. So either I suck it up and take on this new tourism venture, or it doesn't get done. Either way, my exploration-focused vision for Blue Planet Expeditions is never going to happen."

"No," said Stockton. "I just don't see how we can do it inside OceanGate."

"Yeah. Me neither. That sucks."

"Sorry."

Fall 2012

Miami, Florida

I WALKED INTO THE LARGE CONFERENCE ROOM AND LOOKED OUT OF THE floor-to-ceiling windows onto the streets of downtown Miami just two floors below. I heard Stockton follow me in and close the door, so I sat down facing him. I could see through the windows behind him into the open office space where our team was busy at their desks. I knew that this was going to be the first contentious conversation he and I had ever had as co-founders. I also knew it was all my fault for creating a toxic situation that pushed him too far.

"We need to talk," he started before he finished taking his seat. He had just flown in from Seattle, and we had barely even said hello to each other.

"Yeah," I said.

"What the hell is your problem?"

"What do you mean?" I replied, even though I knew full well what he was talking about.

"Your emails," he said. "What's gotten into you? You're so damned condescending." It was not the first time I had been accused of that. As it turned out, it would not be the last, either.

"I didn't mean to be," I said. A complete lie.

"Well, then you just give bad email," he half-joked. "I mean, you're basically trying to teach me about fundraising like I'm a beginner who's never done this before. Who do you think has raised all of our money so far? Not you! Who do you think the investors have bet on? Not you! Who do you think new investors will bet on? Not you!"

"Yeah, well, you wanted to be CEO, so I'm just trying to be a good COO and support your efforts." I continued my lie.

"No, you're not," he said. "You're trying to be a pain in my ass. So let me ask you again: What's your problem?"

"My problem? You're the one who seems to have a strange definition of the CEO role," I said. "You basically took the title, you demoted me to COO, and for the past few weeks, you've just been expecting me to continue doing my same job. Except now you want me to do everything exactly the way you want it. It's like I'm your glorified secretary. Like I said in my emails, if you want the title of CEO, then you have to start acting like a CEO."

Even as the words left my mouth and entered my own ears, I could hear how stupid—and petty—I sounded. What a jerk!

"That's your friggin' job!" he yelled. "And, by the way, you're being a condescending asshole again."

"Yeah."

"You've got to stop this. Right now."

He got up and started pacing. Clearly, he had been thinking about this during the entire flight across the country. I had been thinking about this for weeks.

"Not to rehash our decision, but I thought you didn't even want to be CEO," I said. "I thought you wanted to be involved only part-time, so you could spend time with your family and other business commitments. I thought you wanted me to run the company while you dealt with the board and investors from the chair position."

"You don't want to rehash it, but you're rehashing it anyway," he said. "No, I didn't want to be CEO. I don't want to work on the company full-time. I'd rather focus on other things. But this is too important. And I'm convinced that we won't succeed unless I step in, just like we planned and agreed."

"What about Wendy?" I asked.

"She's okay with it," he said. "The kids are doing much better now, and she knows how much I love this stuff. Besides, we've put enough of our families' money into this that we may as well put more time into it." Given similar conversations I had had with my own wife over the years, I doubted that his wife was being as supportive as he claimed, but I was willing to give him the benefit of the doubt.

"Look, I told you from the beginning that it wasn't a good idea to keep a former co-founder/CEO in the company when another co-founder takes over," I said. "That was the only flaw in our succession plan."

"And I told you that I don't agree with that," he replied. "You don't have to leave. I don't want you to leave. I need you to help me run the company. I need you to help me through this transition. There's still so much work to do. We're just getting started."

"Stockton, we just have completely different leadership and management styles," I said. "I've been told several times that I'm a great leader but a horrible manager, mostly because I give people so much leeway that most times they feel they don't get enough direction from me. You're the complete opposite. You're a micromanager and want everything done exactly your way. The problem is that I don't like being managed like that. I like having the freedom to do things my way."

"Well, your way is not always right."

"Maybe," I said. "But in those cases, I guess I've just gotten used to being the CEO and reporting up to a board. I'm not used to reporting to a boss. And I certainly don't like reporting to a boss who's also a micromanager."

"Well, I'm the one under pressure with the investors, so it's my ass on the line, not yours."

"That's why we made the switch."

"So again, what's your problem?" he asked.

This is the part I had been agonizing over for the past few

weeks. After a lot of painful soul-searching, I had concluded that it was mostly an issue with my ego.

I had enjoyed being CEO of OceanGate, both inside the company with our team and also outside with the media and general public. I liked how it sounded: "CEO of OceanGate." Even though we had previously agreed that I would stay in the role only through the first phase of our company, over time I had grown to believe that it was the last job I would ever have. As superficial as it was, I did not like how the role swap looked to the outside world. "COO of OceanGate" just did not carry the same weight, especially for a former CEO. We could spin it however we wanted, but in the months since we crafted our succession plan, to me it had begun to feel like a demotion. It felt like I had been judged and deemed unworthy to take the company to the next level.

Not that I disagreed with that assessment. After all, fundraising was not my greatest strength as an entrepreneur. Stockton had raised all of the money up to that point, and most likely he would have to raise the millions we would need for the engineering we were planning. I also knew that investors at that early stage mostly bet on the CEO more than on the technology or the business idea. For the next phase of our development, they would want to bet on a CEO who knew engineering. That was Stockton, not me. Intellectually, I knew this. Emotionally and psychologically, it was a tough pill for my fragile ego to swallow. I felt all of this even though we had already decided two years prior that this would happen and had implemented that decision a few months ago. I knew that I had been completely unprofessional in the way I had lashed out at him with my flurry of emails these past few days.

And yet I could not bring myself to admit any of this out loud to Stockton. At least not on that day in that Miami conference room.

"I don't know what my problem is," I said. "Maybe I'm just having a tough time seeing where I fit in after we make this transition."

"What do you mean? COO."

"Exactly, Chief Operating Officer, but we won't be operating, will we?" I said. "We'll be designing and building our new subs. We'll be tearing down *Lula* to rebuild it while also testing the carbon fiber hull for the deep sub. We won't be diving *Antipodes* any more. In other words, no operations."

"But there's still so much more to do."

"We'll be completely overhauling the team," I said. "We'll need to keep some who can help on the engineering side and let go of everyone else. Then we'll need to hire a bunch of new engineers."

"Exactly," he said. "So I need you to manage all of that."

"And we'll be relocating back to Seattle," I continued. "I can't move my family back there. We just got here."

"You can go back and forth," he said. "The flights aren't that bad."

"And we can't justify continuing to pay my salary," I said. "I mean, for my $10K a month we could get a kick-ass engineer in Seattle. That'd be a much better use of funds."

"You don't have to leave."

"I don't want to," I said. I took a moment, knowing that once I uttered the next words, I could not take them back. "But I think I have to."

Stockton sat down again. He had obviously prepared for this outcome.

"Okay, fine," he said. "So how do you want to do this?"

And, just like that, my time at OceanGate came to an end.

We talked for a few more minutes to make some plans about how to break the news to the rest of the team and how to communicate it to the investors and the media. We decided that my last day would be January 31, 2013. Despite our heated exchange, this part of the conversation was incredibly calm and professional, even friendly. Almost like we both knew the importance of the moment.

For me, I would have to figure out what to do next with my life. For Stockton, he would have to figure out how to take over the entire company by himself. I was not sure which of us had the more difficult road ahead.

January 2013
Parkland, Florida

MY LAST DAY AT OCEANGATE WAS COMING UP SOON. I STILL WAS NOT sure exactly what I was going to do next. I think I was not yet accepting the fact that I would be leaving OceanGate, so a big part of me was in denial. Despite my procrastination, I knew I was simply avoiding the hard truth that in a few days I would become the "co-founder and *former* CEO/COO of OceanGate."

I did not necessarily want to do another startup, but I was also not necessarily employable. I thought about staying in the ocean world by getting a job with one of the other sub companies. There just were not enough opportunities to go around. Besides, most of those companies saw OceanGate as a competitor, so they would not want to hire me. I also thought about going back into the space world, but at that point I had been away for almost three years, and it was still as nascent as the day I stepped away. Again, there were just not enough opportunities to go around.

I needed to figure out something. Fast.

I knew enough about startups to know that I could not do another one unless it was something I was passionate about. The easiest thing to do would be to launch a new ocean-focused venture, but it would have to be something that was complementary to OceanGate and not competitive with it.

I revisited my old proposal for Blue Planet Expeditions and tweaked it a bit. Obviously, I would need Stockton's blessing, so I prepared myself for the conversation I would need to have with him during our next call.

"So have you decided what you're going to do next month?" he asked.

"I have some ideas, which is why I wanted to talk," I replied. "I need to run one of them past you."

"Go for it."

"Remember my proposal for Blue Planet Expeditions that we discussed a few months ago?"

"Yup."

"Well, I was thinking of doing that as a new startup. Not as an OceanGate subsidiary, but as a stand-alone venture. We already decided it'd be too much of a distraction inside OceanGate, so I thought maybe I'd do it on my own. Whaddya think?"

"So you'd go start a new company called Blue Planet Expeditions to do ocean exploration expeditions using manned subs?"

"Well, not specifically Blue Planet Expeditions," I said. "It turns out there are a ton of companies with 'Blue Planet' in the name, and also 'Expeditions' seems too generic. I did a little branding exercise, and I'm thinking maybe Blue Marble Exploration."

"That's a good name. But you'd organize expeditions using subs?"

"Yeah. Specifically for exploration."

"No tourism?" he asked.

"Hell no! I'd like to try doing those first-time exploration missions that are too risky to have anyone other than the professional crew involved."

"So what's the revenue model?"

"Sponsorships and media licensing."

"That's it?"

"Yup," I said. "I still think about our conversations with David de Rothschild, and I think he was right. I think there's an opportunity to sell sponsorships, not just to cover the costs of the expeditions but actually to make a profit. In that case, the media licensing revenue would be just icing on the cake, since the real value of the documentaries would be to promote the company and the expeditions. It could be a new template for explorers to use in all sorts of exploration expeditions, not just underwater."

"I'm skeptical, but it's certainly worth a shot. How are you going to get through the initial sales cycle?"

"That's the part I haven't figured out yet. I'll probably need to go out and raise some seed funding from investors. I haven't figured out how much yet, but it shouldn't be too much since we'll probably keep the core team really small. The expedition team will be all project-based contractors, so the sponsor deals should pay for that."

"So no tourism, no citizen science, no Mission Specialists?"

"Nope. None of that."

"So you would never compete with us if at some point we wanted to launch OceanGate Expeditions to do the kinds of missions you and I talked about a while back?"

"Nope. First, you already know that I have no personal desire to do those kinds of expeditions. Second, why would I want to compete with OceanGate? I'll still be a shareholder, right?"

"Yeah," Stockton confirmed. "So same thing with hiring anyone away from the OceanGate team, right?"

"Well, not anyone you want to keep. But if you decide to let go of some ops people, then yeah, I'd want to hire them if I had the money for it. Of course, I'd clear it with you first."

"What about *Titanic*?" Stockton asked. "Would you organize expeditions there? Since we talked, I've been running some numbers, and I think that idea may be worth revisiting at some point, even if DOE decides they don't want to charter our deep subs."

"First, double 'hell no!' on *Titanic*. I have absolutely zero interest in that. Plus, it's not exploration, so it'd be completely off-brand for this new venture."

"Makes sense."

"Wait. So you've been running numbers on *Titanic*?" I was surprised.

"Yeah, well, like we talked about, we're going to need early customers for the deep subs. We already know that the pointy end of the Technology Adoption Curve will be tourists, especially anyone leaning more toward adventure tourism or experiential tourism, so why not look at *Titanic*? After all, there is already an established market for that and a proven model for the sub dives.

All we have to do is shoehorn the Mission Specialist concept into the expeditions."

"I don't know if DOE would want to do that," I said. "You'd have to convince Rob and his team."

"Well, I've also been thinking that they're overcharging for their current experience and leaving money on the table for a different experience," Stockton explained. "I still can't believe that people would pay $20K to $60K for a two-hour visit to the *Titanic*. However, if you offered them a chance to be an active participant in a scientific expedition to document and study the wreck, then you could probably charge $100K or more."

"I could see that. I just don't know if DOE would change their model."

"Well, then in that case, we'll go ahead with the OceanGate Expeditions subsidiary and do it ourselves," said Stockton. "If we can sell enough Mission Specialist slots, not only will it cover the costs of the expedition but we may also help subsidize the test phase of the deep subs. We'll just take the subs there during their experimental phase, since we'll need to do a bunch of test dives anyway. That could even be part of our pitch to the Mission Specialists because in effect, they'd be like test pilots for our new subs. In fact, we could even get the foundation involved in case some of them prefer to make a charitable donation for the science components."

"It sounds like you've been doing a lot more than just crunching numbers," I said.

"Well, I need to stay focused on the *Lula* refit and developing the carbon fiber hull, but our conversation about your Blue Planet Expeditions idea did get me thinking a bit."

"So how do you feel about my Blue Marble Exploration idea? Would you be okay if that's what I did after leaving OceanGate?"

"Would you charter our subs for your expeditions?" he asked.

"That would be my first preference, but we'd have to pick the subs that best align with our mission objectives. For example, for the Dean's Blue Hole expedition, *Antipodes* would be a great fit since we'll be going into a relatively circular cavern and the sub's twin domes could be ideal. For other targets, we might have to use a Triton sub. Or a Nuytco sub. Or some other sub. Whatever works best for the particular mission. We'll need to be sub-agnostic."

"I guess that makes sense," he said. "We can always give you the 'OceanGate co-founder preferred rate' on your charters."

"That'd be great. Then hopefully in the very near future, you'll have your first charter customer for exploration expeditions. Maybe by the end of this year?"

"Sounds good."

"So I can go ahead with this?"

"Yeah, what the hell," he replied. "I'm going to be busy with the engineering work in Seattle anyway. You might as well be out there trying to create a new paying customer for us."

"Excellent!"

"Just do me a favor and don't announce anything publicly or to the team until after you leave," he said.

"No worries on that. I probably won't be ready to announce anything for a few months anyway."

"Okay, well, in that case, I look forward to working together again soon."

"Thanks, Stockton," I said. "I appreciate it."

Chapter 11

ANNIVERSARY

June 2024

Everett, Washington

I GAZED INTO THEIR MANY FACES, APPROXIMATELY FORTY OF THEM, LOOKing past me across Puget Sound over Whidbey Island and toward the sunset. The group had gathered to celebrate the one-year anniversary of our shared loss, when the deep ocean took the lives of the five explorers most of us knew well. Several of us took turns stepping in front of the group and saying a few words. Then we all laid down some flowers and placed a memorial rock along the water's edge. After many hugs and tears, we walked slowly back to the bar to toast our fallen colleagues and bid each other farewell.

A few months prior, Renata Rojas had decided she did not want to be alone on that sad day, so she had planned to travel from her home in New York to Seattle. She wanted to have a quiet lunch at a restaurant near the old OceanGate headquarters, and she wanted to share that special moment with the few people in the world who knew her pain. She invited some of her fellow *Titanic* Mission Specialists, along with some of the OceanGate crew she had come to know as family. She was not sure if anyone would join her, but she was wrong.

Stockton spoke to me often of Renata, affectionately referring to her as "Mission Specialist Zero." She was a diver, an explorer, and a lifelong *Titanic* aficionado. She dreamed for years of seeing the famed shipwreck, and she finally got her wish during one of OceanGate's missions using *Titan*. She was not a wealthy individual who could easily afford the published ticket price for a seat on the crew as a Mission Specialist, so she used her savings to pay for what she thought was the opportunity of a lifetime. Stockton saw something special in her, and he offered her the opportunity to join several expeditions as part of the operations team. She was all too eager to accept and worked like crazy to make sure she added value to every mission. She went on to become one of OceanGate's most ardent advocates and vocal supporters.

She and I spoke for the first time during a call after the accident. She could barely make it through the conversation without breaking down crying. She had been in charge of securing the titanium hatch on *Titan*, so she was the last person to see its crew alive. She was tormented by that memory and tortured by that singular pain.

We had many more conversations in the months leading up to the anniversary, but I did not meet her in person until a few hours prior to the gathering. Although she was still suffering, I sensed she was happy that later in the afternoon she would be in the warm company of her extended family.

By the time I arrived at the local restaurant that evening, many of the guests were already there. Most of them knew each other because they had served together on OceanGate's expeditions and even dived together in *Titan*. They had not seen each other in a year or more, and it was clear, even to an outsider, the warmth that they felt for each other.

Yes, I was an outsider at an OceanGate gathering.

I knew a couple of OceanGate team members and one of the Mission Specialists, and I had met Renata earlier that day. Otherwise, I did not know anyone there. After all, I had left the company a decade prior and had not joined any of the *Titanic* expeditions.

However, Renata had prepared me for the fact that everyone seemed to know who I was, either because I was Stockton's co-founder or because I had been in the media after the accident. I spent a few hours before and after the informal ceremony meeting as many of these wonderful people as I could, hearing their stories, and basking in their passion for exploration. Each of them thanked me for the role I played at the very beginning of OceanGate, and I thanked them for the role they played at the end. They all contributed immensely to the vision Stockton and I had when we started the company.

Obviously, they were all sad about the tragic loss of life. However, they were also sad about OceanGate ceasing operations, about its journey of exploration coming to a halt, and about its culture of technology innovation likely being pushed into obscurity. The negative press leading up to the anniversary was once again attacking everyone involved with OceanGate, and it was frustrating to think that all of the sacrifices may have been in vain.

As I prepared to leave, one of the Mission Specialists shook my hand and said, "Don't ever let anyone convince you this was a failure. It was a huge success. Look around. Everyone here was deeply impacted by their OceanGate experience. Everyone's lives were made better because of what you and Stockton started. Thank you for what you did so many years ago."

Chapter 12

FENDING OFF WOLVES

October 2016
San Francisco, California

THE SUB WAS FINALLY SECURED, AND WE COULD RELAX. SORT OF. STOCKton was still upset with the way the team had mishandled towing the sub back to the marina. Also, he was exhausted from a long day of difficult diving in the low visibility and high currents around Alcatraz. However, somehow he now had to put all of that aside and get ready to head back into the after-party with the crew, guests, and investors. He and I took in a quiet moment on the dock, standing there looking at *Cyclops*.

"You okay?" I asked.

"It just pisses me off when we take one step forward and two steps back," he said. "They're still making rookie mistakes."

"Well, it's only been a year with the new sub, so they're still figuring it out," I said. "Plus, Lochridge still needs more time to upgrade our ops. He's experienced, but he's not a magician." Stockton had hired David Lochridge to head up our dive operations, and he boasted an extensive résumé that was certain to help take OceanGate to the next level.

"Maybe," he said.

"Hey, at least *Cyclops* and its new LRT system both seem to be working well, even in those high currents," I offered.

"Yeah, at least we've got that going for us," he said. Despite everything that happened that day, I could tell that he had even more on his mind.

"How's everything else going?" I asked. "Any more progress since I saw you last year at the oil rig inspection mission in the Gulf of Mexico?"

"You know how it is, things never go as fast as I want," Stockton replied. "We've got great relationships with UW's APL, Boeing, NASA—everyone. We're testing a bunch of systems on *Cyclops* and the new LRT system, and we're moving well on the carbon fiber design for the deep sub."

"So what's the problem?" I asked.

"Will Kohnen, Patrick Lahey, and the rest of them," he said. "They just don't get it. Cameron doesn't want to talk. I don't understand. They say they're all about innovation, but they're not open to having a meaningful conversation about anything we're doing. They just keep coming back to the same old line about all deep subs needing to be spheres made of titanium. It's like talking to a brick wall."

"Well, they've got their businesses to protect," I said. "Do they still consider us competition?"

"Probably," he admitted. "I'm sure they know that we're not in their same business. We're not going to sell our subs to rich guys. But they're not idiots. I'm sure they also realize that once those rich guys hear that they can charter one of our subs for a few hundred thousand to use for a couple of weeks, they probably won't want to spend a few million to own one of theirs for years."

"And they probably don't like that we haven't reclassed *Cyclops* like *Lula* was," I said.

"Don't get me going on the whole classing thing," he said, exasperated. "I mean, I totally get why they need to class their subs. How else would they convince someone to buy them? Besides, they can bake the cost into the purchase price. But you know that no one who charters one of our subs will ever ask if they are classed. No one even knows what that is!"

"And it has nothing to do with safety," I said.

"Exactly!" he said. "We've spent years creating this corporate culture based on safety, and we go way beyond anything a classing agency would ever require. We don't need a piece of paper from them to tell us that we're safe after also teaching them about why we're safe. And we certainly don't need to pay them for that piece of paper!"

"So let me ask the obvious question: Why do you care what they think?" I probed. "I mean, you don't need approval or permission from Will, Patrick, Cameron, McCallum, Nuytten, or anyone else. So what if they don't like what we're doing or how we're doing it?"

"I don't know," he said. "Maybe it's because I know this isn't good for humanity. These guys are the industry leaders and public ambassadors. This planet is mostly ocean, and we've explored so little of it. We need to have more and more access to it, and these guys are just selling high-priced toys to a small group of rich guys. We can't keep going like this. Humanity deserves better."

I pointed to him and then to me. "Preacher. Choir."

"It's also the hypocrisy that pisses me off," he said. "They pontificate about how they're all about innovation, but then they slam anyone who doesn't do things exactly like they think things should be done. They claim that they're out-of-the-box thinkers, but they're so far in the box, they can't see the box."

"Gee, we haven't heard that before in any other industry," I said sarcastically.

"I know!" he said. "It's just that when it comes to the oceans—or even space—this kind of toxic thinking could potentially kill humanity. No exaggeration. I can totally see how Elon must have bruises on his forehead from banging his head against those walls."

"So we have to keep doing the same, right?" I said. "Like Elon, there's only one way to convince anyone that we're right. We're going to have to prove it by doing it."

"I guess. It'd just be nice to get a little support. Or at least a little less resistance."

"Dream on!"

We laughed. Then we walked out of the marina and made our way back to the after-party. The challenges ahead would still be there tomorrow.

Fall 2017
Panama City, Panama

THE PANAMA CANAL WAS INCREDIBLE, LITERALLY. EVEN THOUGH I HAD been living in Panama off and on for most of the year, I still had trouble believing the sheer volume of ships and cargo that passed back and forth in front of my apartment every day and night. I was there to help run my friend's rainforest conservation project, but being so close to the ocean every day just made me miss OceanGate and our sub dives.

My phone rang.

"Hey, Stockton!" I said. "I was just thinking about you."

"Nothing good, I'm sure," he said. "Where are you on this fine day? Atlanta? Panama? The rainforest?"

"In my Panama apartment, watching the ships go in and out of the canal," I said. "Just another Tuesday."

"How's life on the other side of the divorce canal?"

"Not too bad, all things considered," I said. "I mean, everything went so smoothly, amicably, and quickly that now whenever we hit a little bump it just feels weird. Start to finish in six months. I guess we both felt it was time, but mostly we wanted to protect the kids."

"Yeah, that's the important thing," he said. "How are they taking it?"

"Well, they're eighteen, sixteen, and twelve, so it's hitting each of them differently," I said. "Rebecca is off to college and Daniel is focused on his soccer, so Caleb is the one who's most impacted. He's going back and forth between us. We're trying to make it as easy as possible for him."

"Sounds sickeningly healthy."

"Thanks," I said. "How are Wendy and the kids?"

"Good, all things considered," he said. "She's running the foundation now and coming out on our dives. She's actually enjoying the work, and she's even doing our surface comms. It makes things a lot easier on the home front."

"And the kids?"

"All good, all grown," he said. "Ben is working as an engineer and flying. Quincy is off to law school. I don't know who I'm more proud of—him for being a lot like me or her for being nothing like me. She's got inner strength I don't think I could ever have."

"I still can't believe that I've never met her."

"Someday," he assured me.

"So, how's life at OceanGate?" I asked. "I saw the latest shareholder update. It sounds like you're making progress on the carbon fiber."

"Well, as always, one step forward, two steps back," he said. "We're learning more with every iteration. We're getting better at the whole process, and we're improving the strain gauge system."

"Are you still confident that the carbon fiber hull will work?"

"Definitely," he said. "We're working through the four big problems, right? The carbon fiber itself needs to be really thick to handle the pressure, but even at its thickest it will still be lighter and cheaper than titanium, so we've got lots of wiggle room there. The manufacturing process is getting better with every iteration, since we have to make sure that we eliminate any gaps in the layers, but that's a matter of practicing over and over again with multiple hulls, so it will just take time. The biggest challenge is the same one that Graham had with *Challenger*, which is the interface between the carbon fiber hull and the titanium domes, since they handle pressure differently, but we're on a good path to fix that one, too. So it all comes down to the long-term problem, which is that we don't know how many cycles we'll get out of each hull, since it weakens with every dive, but I still think that our computer models and strain gauge system will let us dive safely without ever coming close to the limit on cycles."

"All sounds like great progress, right?" Even though I had seen Stockton butt heads with lots of engineers over the years, I had always been impressed with how many he could convince with his approach to design, testing, and analysis. Of course, there were always people who refused to believe he was right, but then again, that seemed to always be the case with innovators. I had seen that in other industries, such as software, aviation, space, and even economics. Experts always had their own way of thinking that sometimes kept them from being open-minded. Honestly, Stockton was no different, but his singular focus on carbon fiber was also turning Graham's original crazy idea into a reality—slowly but surely.

"Well, we lowered our target to 4,000 meters, and I'm sure we can hit that with more than enough buffer for safety," he said.

"It's just a matter of how much time it'll take us to get there, right?"

"And how much money," he said. "If we can't get past all of this testing and start diving, we'll have to raise more money. It wouldn't be the end of the world, but always asking for money is a pain in the ass. Plus it's a huge distraction."

"But we need to have enough runway to make sure we do this right," I said. "Our current investors understand that. At least you've been setting the right expectations with your shareholder updates and the annual shareholder meetings."

"Yeah, but still. I'd prefer to be diving than testing. We didn't start this company to test. We started it to explore."

"I know, I know," I said. "What about ramping up charter operations with *Antipodes* and *Cyclops*? They're off-brand, but they could also potentially bring in some revenue."

"We've looked into that, too," he said. "I'd rather sell *Antipodes*, which you know we've been trying to do. We've gotten close with a few folks, but then they just fall apart."

"I know this goes against our founding vision, but have you considered just giving up on the deep sub?" I asked. "Maybe we throw in the towel on carbon fiber and just try building our business model around our two current subs? Yeah, they're old, heavy, and shallow, but at least we could explore near coastlines. We'd be leaving the deep ocean and heading back to shore."

"No, we can't go back," he said, his voice firm. "We've come too far and made too much progress. Plus, we're so close! I'm absolutely 100 percent convinced that we'll figure out how to use carbon fiber for deep ocean work. Once we prove it out, maybe twenty years from now, all deep subs in the world will be made of carbon fiber. We have to keep going."

"So we're back to fundraising, the one thing you hate almost as much as giving up," I joked.

"Yeah, it beats the alternative."

Stockton was stubborn, but I had enough experience with entrepreneurs to know that there was a fine line separating that from perseverance. He had always been willing to be turned around on any topic, but by the time we hung up that day, I got the feeling that he had mentally crossed over to the other side. We were committed to building new deep subs using cylindrical carbon fiber hulls.

One way or another, Stockton was going to make it happen. No one and nothing could stop him.

Fall 2018

San Francisco, California

SFO WAS TYPICALLY CROWDED ON FRIDAYS, SO I WAS RELIEVED THAT I got to my gate two hours before my flight started boarding. It had already been a whirlwind "West Coast Swing," and I was eager to get some rest over the weekend at home in Atlanta before heading right back out to LA on Monday morning.

I had just found a relatively quiet spot to sit down and reply to some emails, when my phone rang.

"Hey, Stockton!" I said. "Miss me already?"

"Ha! Yeah, it's been, what, three days?"

"Thanks again for the great dive day on Tuesday," I said. "I know that Jonathan and the rest of the gang loved it. Plus it's good that you got to spend some quality time with them. They really appreciated it. Kellie took a bunch of photos, so I'm sure she'll be sending them out soon."

"It was a good group," he said. "I'm glad we got two good dives in."

"And great weather," I added. "I still remember what you said when I first moved to Seattle: 'Seattle has two seasons. Winter and August.' So true!"

"Well, I'm glad it all worked out," he said. "You're at the airport, right? Do you have some time before your flight?"

"Yup. What's going on?"

"You and I didn't get to talk much, and I need your thoughts on this whole Lochridge thing."

"Ugh! Sure. What's the latest on all that?"

"It's a mess," he said. "Now he filed a whistleblower complaint with OSHA. He claims that I fired him because he said the sub was unsafe and because he wrote that damn report. The lawyers want me to sue him for breaching his confidentiality agreement. At this point, I just want him to go away so we can keep working. Maybe we should go after him just so he'll settle?"

"Are you asking me or telling me?"

"I don't know," he said. "I just get pissed off whenever I think of him. What's your take on all of this?"

"Geez, where to start?" I said. "I already told you before that I've never had to deal with an employee situation like this. I mean, you hired him to do a job he was qualified for, you asked him to do something that was in his job description, he refused to do it, and then he tried doing another job that he was not qualified for, that he had not been hired for, and that someone else was already doing. All of this knowing that the company was on a tight timeline and couldn't afford too many hiccups."

"And don't forget he tried squeezing us for his work visa," he said. "He told me that I couldn't fire him because he had brought his family over from Scotland."

"And that," I said. "In the Marine Corps, this would be considered a crime. It's a violation of Article 92 of the Uniform Code of Military Justice. It's refusing to follow a lawful order from a commanding officer. You'd get court-martialed and potentially thrown in the brig and kicked out of the Marine Corps. Of course you could claim that the order was unlawful, but that's a defense at your trial. You still get court-martialed. And that's something a judge or jury would decide, so you run the risk that they disagree with you and decide it was a lawful order. Then you're screwed. Of course, in the civilian world, it's not a crime to refuse to do something your boss tells you to do, but you have to accept the risk that you could get fired. You can always complain about it later, but you still get fired."

"Well, that's what he's doing now," he said. "Even though I tried over and over to work with him. Hell, I needed him to stay on. He was a great ops guy. We needed him to get the sub diving. I didn't want to fire him. He just thought he knew better than the engineering team and wouldn't stay in his box."

"And nothing he was pointing out was new stuff, right?"

"No! The engineering team had already gone over everything he listed in his report and was comfortable with it," he said. "It's like he took it upon himself to make a stand in the name of safety, but then he just pointed out stuff we already knew. He was playing engineer, which he's not. He's an ops guy."

"He was definitely a great ops guy," I said. "I really liked him. It's too bad he didn't work out. He would've been amazing on *Titan*."

"I just don't know what I could've done differently," he said.

"Well, I've always thought that the whistleblower laws are a strange gray area," I offered. "I mean, I know why they exist. However, from the perspective of a manager, it gets dicey because there's a fine line between getting rid of someone because they're pointing out safety concerns and getting rid of someone because they're not a good fit for the organization. As you know, I've always thought that this conflict between you and Lochridge came down to you needing an ops guy with the mentality of a test pilot to take *Titan* through its experimental phase, but instead, it turns out that he's got the mentality of an airline pilot. He may be a great ops guy, but maybe he's just not the right person for this stage of R&D. Then again, I've never really spoken with him directly on this, so I'm only hearing your side of the story, right?"

"Yeah, except his side of the story is bullshit," he said.

"I can't help you with that, because I have no idea what I would've done if I was in his shoes," I said. "I don't think I would've challenged you like he did, mostly because of my Marine Corps training and knowing how to stay in my lane. I also don't think I would've resigned in protest. I probably would've voiced my concerns and signed off on the transfer from engineering, but then I would've created a rigorous test dive plan that allowed me to verify every one of my concerns while wearing the ops hat you hired me to wear. Then again, I haven't seen his report and haven't spoken with him, so I don't know exactly." A part of me wished I was still at the company to help broker a truce between them.

"Yeah, well, now I've got to figure out how to push forward with ops while also dealing with this OSHA complaint," he said. "It's just a distraction we don't need right now. You know how much I hate spending money on lawyers, but it might be the only way to close this up."

"Hmmm. Not to pile on, but what's going on with Will Kohnen, Patrick Lahey, and the whole MTS crowd?"

"You mean that letter?" he said. "They never sent it, and I never saw it. I talked with Will about it. I still can't believe they wasted time writing that thing. I mean, we've been talking about all of their issues for years. I went to UI and shared with them what we're doing. I asked for their help. I even hired Will to do some work for us. But all they can do is keep saying the same things over and over again."

"They see us as competition, and they're stuck inside their box," I said. "We've talked about this a million times. We don't need them, right? They'll probably just file away that letter in some drawer, in case they need to pull it out someday and cover their asses. Why do you let it get to you?"

"Well, now they're just pissing me off," he said. "Like we've said before, the only way to win is to go out and prove them wrong."

"But that's the frustrating thing," I said. "They have so much skill and experience that they could really help us make a difference in the world. I completely understand that it's not their business model and so it doesn't make sense for them to do what we're doing. I could even accept them not wanting to help us because it would be a distraction for them or maybe they even see it as helping a potential competitor. But to actively try preventing us from going after this? At a minimum, that stinks of anticompetitive behavior. Worse, it's not helping humanity."

"Well, screw them," Stockton declared. "From here on out, it looks like we're on our own."

Chapter 13

IMPOSTOR

September 2024
Barcelona, Spain

"YOU'RE A DOC GUY," HE SAID.

I'm a what? I thought. Instead, I asked, "What do you mean?"

"I think of you as one of the guys producing a documentary," he said. "Your team is trying to get access to our footage, just like Netflix and everyone else."

This hit me like a ton of bricks. I did not know why, but my head was instantly reeling. A flurry of thoughts suddenly filled my mind, and I struggled to continue a coherent conversation.

I was on the phone with Gordon Gardiner, the CEO who had been hired by the board in the immediate aftermath of the accident to replace Stockton. He had been thrust into an unimaginable situation, and he had done an admirable job balancing the needs of the company to shut down operations with the needs of the team members and families of the victims to mourn their loved ones. With no previous knowledge or experience in the submersible world, he had to quickly educate himself while also collaborating with multiple investigations and pending litigation. It was a tall order for any business executive, and he had certainly risen to the occasion.

Of course, for me, his hiring presented a unique challenge because he did not know me from a hole in the wall.

He was certainly aware that I was Stockton's co-founder. Likewise, he had seen me in the media over the past year or so. However, he also knew that I had been out of the company for over a decade, that I had only a very minor ownership interest in the company, and that very few of the current board members, investors, team, or Mission Specialists had ever met me. Even though he and I had introduced ourselves once in person during one of my visits to Seattle, I imagined that to him I was just a name on the spreadsheet that listed OceanGate's shareholders.

Through his perspective, I could see how he would view me as "a doc guy." Even though he and I had communicated extensively about various topics, including the board, how Wendy and the kids were faring, the decision to shut down operations, the team, the memorial service, finding a buyer for *Cyclops*, the investigations, and other issues, by far most of our interactions had to do with the documentary project on which I was an advisor and technical consultant. I appreciated how he could see it as "my" project, even though I was not one of the producers and I played only a minor role.

The sickening jab I felt when he called me a doc guy was

unexpected, and it took me a few days of soul-searching to figure out why it had hit me so hard.

In the heat of the moment, I did manage to stammer something about the documentary not being my project. I also squeaked out something about my being the co-founder and not merely a doc guy. Recognizing he had inadvertently struck a nerve, he graciously heard me out and tried to appease me, but even I could feel that this was not his problem—it was mine.

After we hung up, I spent quite some time reflecting on the exchange.

My thoughts took me all the way back to the moment I first heard the news about the surface ship losing communications with the sub. Even as I scoured news headlines on my phone while walking through Vienna, I was already thinking about the situation as if I was still at the company. I thought of different options on how I could help, including providing shoreside support for the search and rescue operations, coordinating a public response with the board and PR firm, speaking with Wendy or other members of the team, and even potentially flying to St. John's, the launching point for the expedition, in case I could find my way onto the support ship.

I very much considered OceanGate *my* company.

Even though I had not worked there since 2013, I was still one of its co-founders. It was still mine and Stockton's. Entrepreneurs always view their startups like their children, and co-founders are always their parents, even after they've grown up and left the nest or even if they become estranged. Over the years, Stockton and I had kept in touch, so I felt like I was updated on how our "child" was doing. I still felt like I was part of the company, and I felt like I could still play an important role.

As the search and rescue operation continued through those first few days and as I began to accept that the crew had actually been killed during an implosion, I prepared myself for the reality of losing Stockton. Given that no one from the OceanGate team had stepped forward as a public spokesperson that week, I determined that we likely had no succession plan in place for the death of our CEO. The company would need a leader, and I did not think that any of the current board members would step in. There would be a void during a difficult time, and someone would need to fill it.

What if Wendy calls me to come back as CEO? I had thought. If the board asked me, I would probably decline. After all, I had a full plate of responsibilities across my various ventures, and I had just relocated to Barcelona and did not want to move back to Seattle. However, I would not be able to say no to my friend's widow.

After the press conference announcing the implosion, I braced myself for the call. It never came.

A few weeks later, Gordon sent out an email to all OceanGate shareholders to discuss a number of topics. He introduced himself as the new CEO. At the time, I was relieved that we had found someone else to take us through this difficult time. I was off the hook and could continue focusing on my own life.

It wasn't until my "doc guy" conversation with him a year later that I recalled a nagging thought in the recesses of my brain: *Why him and not me?* After all, it was my company, right? Mine and Stockton's. I would think that I would be the natural first call that Wendy or the board would make. I was certain that I would have been the first call that Stockton would have made.

I did not realize it had bothered me that much until it hit me later.

Maybe it was my ego? Probably. Certainly it was my parental instinct with my baby, OceanGate. There was also a more logical business rationale, because as a shareholder, I would have preferred the board to bring in someone who knew the industry, the company, and the extended team. Who better than the company's co-founder?

At the time, I did not think much about this, but it was clearly percolating in the background of my psyche.

A few months later, when Renata Rojas wanted to introduce the documentary production team to some of her fellow Mission Specialists, she mentioned that having me as a consultant on the project was not necessarily a selling point. To most of the crew from the *Titanic* expeditions, I was essentially a complete stranger. They knew who I was, but they had never met me, and they knew I had never been on one of their expeditions. They considered me an outsider. Worse, they considered me opportunistic, because they thought I was popping back into the company just to use my role as co-founder to benefit the documentary project.

That was definitely a gut punch. Actually, it pissed me off, for so many reasons, and I let Renata know it, too.

I was the company's co-founder, so my personal and professional reputation would always be tied to OceanGate. If anything, I had more of a vested interest in doing right by the company than anyone else on the planet, except, of course, Wendy. I could not believe that anyone who had been with the company only recently would even dare question my loyalty or my motives.

Also, for weeks and months following the accident, I had

provided a full-throated defense of Stockton and OceanGate in the media, which led to my public harassment and a complete derailment of my life. Everyone was mourning the loss, but I was mourning while also getting slammed publicly. This was certainly my own decision, and I had to live with the consequences of that decision, but again, it bothered me that anyone would question my loyalty or my motives.

Finally, I felt that everyone was forgetting what it meant to be a co-founder. If I had not done what I did with Stockton at the start of the company, then none of this would have been possible. None of the Mission Specialists would have ever had the opportunity to serve as crew on any expeditions, including the *Titanic*. I felt that that early effort and sacrifice would be sufficient to preclude ever being considered an outsider in my own company.

That exchange with Renata made me mad, but not at her, since she was merely the messenger. Not even with the Mission Specialists who had made those comments to her. There was something deeper going on, but I could not put my finger on it.

Until the "doc guy" conversation with Gordon a few months later.

It was my frail ego. It was my having to face reality versus my own perception. It was my feeling like an impostor, that I really was not someone I thought I was. It was feeling that I was more important than I really was.

Making this self-discovery was jarring but also strangely liberating. It meant that I did not have to feel burdened by a sense of responsibility for everything related to OceanGate. It meant that I could finally find a balance between the accident's aftermath and my current life.

This was tested again during the US Coast Guard's public hearings.

I had been subpoenaed to testify virtually from Spain, and I was scheduled for one and a half hours. I emailed one of the investigators, offering to testify for three hours, in case they needed me to provide more context for the other witnesses. Reviewing the witness list, it was clear that the panel would need someone to provide some unbiased context, and I thought I was the only one on the list who could fill that role. Apparently, the panel did not agree because they never replied to my offer. Like I said, apparently I thought I was more important than I actually was.

Despite this blow to my ego, I knew there was something important I needed to be doing. I knew this because, in the months since the ship lost comms with the sub, I had had Stockton's voice in my head. I asked myself over and over, "What would Stockton do?" Even if the feeling was misplaced, I had felt an ongoing duty to him, his family, the families of the other crew members, the extended OceanGate family, and even the entire ocean exploration and submersible communities.

Impostor or not, I had to keep pushing forward.

Chapter 14

SUCCESS IN THE ATLANTIC

Fall 2021

Zurich, Switzerland

It was unseasonably warm in Zurich, but it was perfect for my 10K run along the river. I was still dripping sweat in my home office when the phone rang. I did the quick math and figured it was 5:30 AM in Seattle.

"You're up early," I said.

"My usual time," Stockton said. "I figured you're the only one I could call at this hour."

"So . . . you did it!" I said. "Congratulations! I saw the announcement."

"We did it!" he said. "Finally!"

"How'd it go?"

"It was a cluster," he admitted. "I'm shocked we even got down there. It seemed like we had problems with everything. The boat, the LARS, the sub. Every time we turned around, something else was going haywire."

"In other words, a typical set of test dives for an experimental sub."

"Yeah, I guess," he said. "It's just frustrating. Every time we fix one thing, something else malfunctions. A few big issues, but mostly small stuff that's just annoying."

"But it's all part of the R&D process," I said. "It's the only way to learn lessons and improve everything."

"Oh, believe me, we learned way too many lessons on this one," he said. "It'll be so much better next year."

"How was the sub?" I asked.

"Again, lots of lessons learned," he said. "Seriously, it was like Whack-a-Mole with all of the components and subsystems, but at least the strain gauge system seems to be working."

"So you're still comfortable with the carbon fiber hull?"

"Yup," he said. "The next one will be even better."

"And the LARS worked well?" I asked.

"Yeah, pretty much," he answered. "This is the third one we've built, so we're getting pretty good at them. The ones for *Antipodes* and *Cyclops* are good enough for those subs, since they tend to dive nearshore. For the *Titan* LARS, we really had to take it up a notch, since that one has to work in the open ocean. From an engineering standpoint, it's solid, and obviously, we have more than enough experience operating these platforms. It's just a matter of testing it in high sea states and seeing how it performs. All good progress."

"But you still used a big ship with a crane, right?"

"Yeah, well, for two reasons," he said. "First, safety. We're still testing that LARS, so I didn't want to go into the open ocean relying only on that system for the launch and retrieval of the sub. Second, even though these are still test dives, we've got Mission Specialists who paid a lot of money to be there, so we figured they deserved some of the creature comforts that a bigger ship would provide. We wanted to make sure they were happy, even if they didn't get to dive on the wreck."

"Wait, how was the wreck itself?" I asked. "Was it as magical as everyone says it is?"

"The bow is really impressive," he said. "We got some nice footage of that section. It's a huge ship. And clearly, it's deteriorating."

"How was the crew?"

"You can imagine," he said. "PH was happy as a clam, and his positive attitude was infectious. Everyone else was grinning ear to ear. The team was relieved that we were able to dive at all, so actually reaching the wreck was a bonus."

"And the Mission Specialists?"

"The ones that made it got their money's worth," he said. "But we'll have to bring some of them back next year."

"All great stuff," I said. "I'm assuming everyone got home okay, and the sub's back in Everett, right?"

"Yup."

"So now what?"

"Lots to fix," Stockton said. "Lots to improve. Then we'll go again next year."

Chapter 15

HEARINGS

September 2024

Charleston, South Carolina

I WAS SWORN IN, AND MY TESTIMONY BEGAN. FOR THE NEXT HOUR AND A half, I fielded questions from members of the US Coast Guard and the National Transportation Safety Board (NTSB) investigation teams. It was the first day of the second and final week of the public hearings for the Marine Board of Investigation regarding the *Titan* incident, and I had been permitted to testify virtually from Barcelona. Given that I had been preparing for a few weeks since I had received my subpoena, there were few surprises.

Actually, for about twenty minutes toward the end of my allotted time, the NTSB investigator probed quite extensively into my interactions with the Coast Guard during my time at OceanGate. He asked several times about how we sought approval for our operations in US waters, how we conformed with Coast Guard regulations, and how we communicated with the various Coast Guard sectors in Washington, California, and Florida. At first, I could not understand why our diving *Antipodes* along the US coastline over a decade ago was in any way relevant to our diving *Titan* in international waters during the *Titanic* expeditions. Then it dawned on me that the NTSB was likely trying to assess whether the Coast Guard could have done anything differently to prevent the accident or if it could do anything differently in the future to avoid similar accidents in domestic waters.

Since I was six hours ahead of Charleston, I did not have the time to watch all of the witnesses testify live. However, over the next few weeks, I managed to watch many of the recorded videos available on the Coast Guard's YouTube channel. It was a frustrating experience.

On the one hand, I was impressed by the panel and by the witness list. The investigators were respectful and professional, and they clearly took their roles seriously in what they repeatedly described as administrative, not legal, proceedings. I was certain that no one on the investigation teams had any experience with the ultra niche field of crewed submersibles, but they had spent the previous year becoming as knowledgeable as could be expected. They had solicited input from a wide variety of sources, they had reviewed extensive amounts of evidence, and they had conducted thorough research. They were clear that the two weeks of public hearings were not the culmination of the investigations, nor did they represent the total extent of the investigations. After all, there were many witnesses—mostly from OceanGate—who had not been allowed to testify publicly because of pending legal matters, including a $50 million wrongful death suit filed in August by the estate of PH Nargeolet. The panel did the best they could to field a lineup of witnesses that was as fair and unbiased as possible under the circumstances, if anything to help create a comprehensive public record.

On the other hand, I was continually frustrated by the lack of proper questioning from the panel. Either they did not have enough expertise to ask the right questions, or they had made a strategic decision not to ask the right questions. Either way, it was not a good showing. Sometimes, it would have been as simple as asking commonsense follow-up questions that did not require any subject-matter expertise. For example, when a witness was shown a list of seven items that had gone wrong during a *Titan* dive, no one bothered to ask if having this many anomalies during a dive was normal. The answer would have been "Of course!" Instead, the public (and perhaps the panel) was left with the impression that the sub was falling apart.

Regardless, I thought every witness was credible and did a solid job of answering questions and presenting powerful closing statements.

I also spent some time reading the public comments during the live testimony. It was clear that several trolls had shown up just to cause trouble with their ignorant drivel and contentious attacks. However, there were also many people who appeared genuinely interested in learning more about what was going on. Unfortunately, it was not the best platform for educating anyone. At several points, some of the witnesses jumped into the comments to try answering valid questions, only to be attacked by the trolls, and eventually giving up.

For me, I was struck the most by the testimonies of Patrick

Lahey on the first Friday and by David Lochridge on the second Tuesday. I knew both men, and I respected both of them, even if they had each fallen out with Stockton. It was difficult for me to hear them testify about how much they disagreed with him and how derisively they spoke about him. It was even harder to accept that he was not alive to defend himself, even if his lawyers would have precluded him from testifying.

At one point, I thought to myself that both Patrick and David came across as professional, knowledgeable, articulate, passionate, and trustworthy. They also seemed like fun guys who people would love to just hang out with. Knowing them, I knew that is exactly what they were like.

Then it hit me: I had also just described Stockton Rush.

I immediately felt a pang of sadness and deep loss. Stockton fought for years to draw the general public's attention to the world of ocean exploration and submersibles. Now that the world was watching, he was not there to be one of the ocean's most passionate ambassadors. Quite the contrary—in his absence, he was being painted as the antithesis of Lochridge and Lahey, when in reality he was almost exactly the same. I thought it was a shame that none of the people watching the hearings would ever get to meet Stockton. At the same time, I felt privileged to have known him.

Several witnesses testified regarding the engineering decisions and testing process that went into the design of *Titan*. All of them seemed to have impeccable credentials that qualified them as subject-matter experts to provide opinions in front of the panel. By contrast, Stockton was depicted as someone who had an aerospace engineering background but clearly did not know what he was doing when it came to submersibles. It made me wonder why no one ever put forth Stockton's credentials as a subject-matter expert. After all, by the time he started designing *Titan*, he had almost a full decade of experience with submersibles.

He began his journey building and diving a two-person "kit" sub he had purchased. Then he collaborated with Graham Hawkes on his design for *Deep Flight 2*. That led to OceanGate purchasing and operating *Antipodes*, which Stockton upgraded. In turn, that led to our purchasing *Lula 500*, which he stripped down and rebuilt as *Cyclops*. Along the way, he even took the initial design for a "Launch, Recovery, and Transport" system from the University of Hawaii and over time evolved it into the open-ocean launch and retrieval system that was used for *Antipodes*, *Cyclops*, and *Titan*. I had never asked Will Kohnen, Patrick Lahey, Karl Stanley, and others, but I wondered how much sub design experience they had when they took on their first major sub build. I could not imagine that it was much more than Stockton had.

Also, at the time of his death, he was probably one of the two most knowledgeable people on the planet about the use of carbon fiber hulls for deep-diving submersibles. The other was Graham Hawkes, who had first introduced Stockton to the idea. Given that the US Navy had built a similar vessel prior, there were probably experts on the military side, but Stockton and Graham were probably the only civilians. Although the investigators knew about Graham, for some reason he did not testify at the hearings.

The bottom line was that Stockton was a highly qualified submersible designer, or at least as qualified as any of the other subject-matter experts who testified as witnesses.

The public hearings concluded, but the investigations continued. It could be months before they concluded and final reports were issued. Not only would the investigators have to compile their process, the evidence, and their findings, but they would also have to make recommendations on how best to move forward and prevent such accidents in the future. It had always been a massive undertaking, and it would take even longer to complete.

I did not watch the replay of my testimony, mostly because I did not want to read the public comments. I could imagine what they said.

Also, I was exhausted from the year-long struggle to change the negative narrative. I certainly did not expect it to turn positive, but I dared to dream that minds might someday open enough to allow a more nuanced view of this tragic event.

Maybe someday. But not during those public hearings.

Chapter 16

UNKNOWN FAREWELL

May 2023

Atlanta, Georgia

MY PHONE RANG, AND STOCKTON'S PHOTO APPEARED IN MY CALLER ID. He and I rarely scheduled calls, and he was one of the few people in my life who could ping me randomly and expect me to pick up. I always enjoyed catching up with him, not just because it brought my mind back to my time at OceanGate but also because I truly enjoyed our conversations. They were intellectually stimulating and full of energy. Also, I liked to think that I was one of the few people Stockton felt would understand whatever issue he was grappling with at the time. He knew he could speak freely with me, and he expected me to give him unvarnished feedback.

"So where in the world am I finding you on this fine day?" he asked. He opened with his boyish enthusiasm. God, it was great to hear his voice.

"Atlanta. What are you up to?" I asked. I already knew the response that was coming, because I had heard it so many times before in our now-familiar opening exchange.

"Same as always. Working my ass off to make your shares worth something someday," he said. I often thought he was only half joking.

"Thanks for that," I said. My usual reply. "Are you still in Seattle?"

"Yeah. I fly out to St. John's tomorrow," he said. "The team's already there, so hopefully everything's moving along nicely."

"How's the expedition shaping up?" I asked.

"Well, I'd love to have sold a few more seats," he said—just like he did every year. "But the sub's looking good, the ship seems like it'll work out fine, and the team's ready. The only fly in the ointment is always the weather. Hopefully it'll cooperate this year."

"How about the Mission Specialists?"

"Great!" he exclaimed. "PH is back, which makes all the difference. And everyone else seems like they'll be a great fit. They all have a great attitude, so hopefully they'll all have a great time, even if they don't get to dive."

"Hey, is Hamish going this year?" I asked. I had met Hamish Harding during a microgravity training flight the previous year, and we had talked extensively about OceanGate, *Titan*, and the *Titanic* expedition. We also discussed his various exploration adventures, especially his world record for circumnavigating the globe in a private jet. Mostly, we talked about his family, especially his son. A few weeks later, I got to meet his wife and son at Hamish's suborbital flight with Blue Origin, where I had been invited as a guest of one of his other crewmates. He was definitely an interesting person with a huge personality and a voracious appetite for life.

"Yup," he replied. "I'm not sure exactly which mission he's on. Somewhere in the middle, I think."

"Nice! I'm sure it'll be great having him on board," I said. "He's quite a character. You'll definitely enjoy having him in the sub."

"So are you going to finally join us this year?" he asked. "As you know, we've got a couple of slots on the first mission."

"I know, I know! I spent the past few days working through a bunch of different travel options," I said. "Unfortunately, I can't find anything that gets me back in time for Caleb's graduation."

"Well, you don't want to miss that," he said. "There will always be other dives, but you've got to be there for your kids. I still can't believe how much mine have grown up!"

"Oh, yeah . . . you're a grandpa!"

"Don't remind me!" he laughed. "I mean, they're amazing and I love them, but I really don't feel old enough to have grandkids."

"Well, I'm bummed I won't be able to join you this year."

"Yeah, me too. Maybe next year?"

"Speaking of next year, and completely shifting topics . . . I know you're trying to focus on the expedition right now, but have you thought any more about what we do next?" I asked. "You've been doing this a long time now. Are we at a point where we can finish the testing phase for *Titan* and finally find you a replacement CEO? Or have we proven out *Titan* to the point that we could potentially sell the company?"

"Nah, I'm still okay being CEO, even though I'm sure Wendy and the kids would love to have me around more," Stockton replied. "And the investors are still okay riding this out a bit longer. Hopefully we work out some of the remaining bugs during this expedition, and then we can raise some more money to build a couple of production-grade subs to replace *Titan*. After that, we can figure out next steps."

"If you're still up for it then, yeah, all that sounds great. If you want, I'm happy to help you do some strategic planning and white-boarding. Maybe I can come out to Seattle after you recover from the expedition?"

"Yeah, let's do it! I'll want to spend August with the family, so maybe in September?"

"Sounds like a plan," I said. "I'll put it on my calendar and follow up with you after you get back. Have a great time on the expedition."

"Will do. See you soon."

We hung up.

It was the last time I would ever speak with Stockton Rush.

Chapter 17

BOOK

December 2024
Barcelona, Spain

My new home office overlooks the Mediterranean. I often find myself transfixed by the dark blue and turquoise waters below my balcony. I imagine the sea flowing west through the Straits of Gibraltar and into the Atlantic Ocean. I know that further on, it also connects to the Pacific. And the Arctic. And the Indian. I know that this planet was sorely misnamed, because it is one large Planet Ocean and not a Planet Earth.

In our hubris, humans believe that this planet was made specifically for us. After all, there are eight billion of us now, and we deem ourselves to be masters of our world. However, 95 percent of us live on only 3 percent of the surface area, mostly along coastlines. Scientists estimate that more than 90 percent of the habitable environment on this planet lies underwater. We just do not think about it in those terms because our bodies are not designed to survive down there.

It does not matter what we think or believe, because the truth is that we are insignificant when compared to the vastness of our oceans. Those oceans do not really care about us. They were here long before we arrived and will remain long after we are gone. They are much more important to the health and well-being of this planet than we are. We are only now starting to understand and appreciate that fact.

For the past year and a half, my life has been turned upside down. I have suffered the loss of a friend, and a company I cherished has effectively disappeared. I willingly threw myself at the mercy of public scrutiny, and I was expectedly gutted. My personal and professional relationships are in distress, my finances are suffering, and my future is uncertain. I know that I willingly chose this path, and I know that my woes are ridiculous compared to the sacrifices of *Titan*'s five crew members and the four families mourning their loss.

I have recurring bouts of survivor's guilt. I cannot help but think that if I had not left OceanGate so many years ago, then perhaps I could have altered the course of our development process and in some way avoided this tragedy and loss of life. My ego likes to think that Stockton respected me as a co-founder and would have listened to me if I had had any concerns. After all, he and I had completely different temperaments, so potentially my more deliberate personality might have offset his more impulsive nature.

Would've, could've, should've. The Holy Trinity of Regret.

I have been frustrated in my efforts to tell the full story of

Stockton, OceanGate, and *Titan*. I have sat for three hours of media interviews, only to have my thoughts cut down to a thirty-second sound bite. I have advised an incredibly compassionate documentary production team, only to realize that my commentary will be only one of dozens that the director will have to weave into a ninety-minute film. I have prepared for weeks to testify before investigators, only to sit through an hour and a half of light questioning. I have been turning my life inside out but with nothing to show for it.

Then, six months ago, it dawned on me that the only way to fulfill my commitment to Stockton and the rest of the crew would be to write a book—this book.

It has been by far the most daunting undertaking of my life. It has consumed me for the past six months, and it will continue to do so until it comes out in print a year from now. However, it seems to be the only way I can get out the entire story. The only way to preserve a legacy more than fifteen years in the making. The only way for humanity to benefit from the many sacrifices made by everyone who ever worked at OceanGate, especially the five members of *Titan*'s final crew.

It has also been a meaningful part of my grieving process. This allowed me to recall an entire history of memories from my friendship and collaboration with Stockton. It provided me an opportunity to revisit the rationale behind so many strategic decisions we made along the way. Most importantly, it reconnected me with the shared passion that led the two of us to start the company so many years ago.

This Planet Ocean is our home. We have to accept that our long-term survival depends on living in balance with it. We cannot protect that which we do not understand; we cannot understand that which we do not study; and we cannot study that which we do not explore. Exploration is the lynchpin of humanity's survival.

Stockton and the other members of *Titan*'s crew embraced this philosophy. They gave up their lives for it.

Critics and naysayers will have us believe that the story of Stockton Rush and *Titan* has ended. They knew it was doomed from the beginning, so the sub's implosion and the five unfortunate fatalities were foregone conclusions. I refuse to accept this. Not only is that an insult to the legacies of five courageous explorers, but also, it is a dangerous precedent to set for the survival of the human species.

Although Stockton, the four crew members, *Titan*, and OceanGate may be gone, their story is just beginning.

The founding vision for our company still remains, because humanity still needs better access to the deep oceans in order to properly explore them. We still need creative innovators developing new technologies, new materials, and new business models to unlock the mysteries of our water world. We still need brave explorers to plunge into the dark depths in search of discovery and in pursuit of inspiration.

I am hopeful that in the near future there will be multiple submersibles around the world made of carbon fiber—or some other material—that will reduce operational costs exponentially while also significantly increasing operational capabilities. Lost in the noise about *Titan*'s implosion was the fact that its fatal dive was actually its thirteenth dive. Stockton's design worked. It needs to be improved, not abandoned.

Whether you liked him or not, agreed with him or not, or got along with him or not, you must admit that Stockton Rush helped push forward the public discussion about technology innovation in the pursuit of ocean exploration for the good of humanity.

Good or bad, Stockton's final story is still being written.

Good or bad, we have not seen the last of *Titan*.

EPILOGUE

Has it really been two years? I can hardly believe that so much time has passed since the accident.

I just realized the other day that this is the longest I have gone without speaking to Stockton. Even after leaving OceanGate more than twelve years ago, I got used to enjoying our occasional conversations. I still talk with him in my head, and sometimes out loud. I wonder what he would think of the tragic implosion and the aftermath.

The title of this book implies that this story will continue to evolve, and it certainly has evolved, even in the six months since I finished the manuscript.

- In March 2025, a tourist submersible operating off the coast of Egypt suffered an accident, and six people (of the thirty-nine on board) lost their lives. Despite the media trying to draw parallels to the *Titan* accident and despite this replacing *Titan* as the record for most fatalities in a private submersible, this event garnered relatively little public attention. The story was out of the news cycle within twenty-four hours. We still know very little about it, including the cause.

- In May and June 2025, BBC/Discovery and Netflix released their documentaries about the *Titan* accident. Neither provided any new information, so they were essentially compilations of everything we had already heard or read in the media over the past two years. The Netflix film actually debuted at #2 on their platform, and at one point I saw a statistic that it had over 200 million streams. I could not believe that so many people would want to watch this kind of documentary, especially considering it received generally poor reviews from critics.
- In June 2025, a small group of us from the extended OceanGate family got together in Seattle for a two-year memorial service. At one point, I looked around and realized that the people gathered spanned the entirety of the company's fourteen-year existence. It was a powerful reminder that despite all the negativity in the media, OceanGate did, in fact, have a positive impact on so many people's lives.
- In July 2025, I spoke with the CEO of a company that has spent the past five years building and operating autonomous submersibles for the US Navy. Their subs use carbon fiber for the pressure vessels, and they have operated dozens of them at depths greater than *Titan*

and for long periods of time, even beyond six months. He is 100 percent convinced that carbon fiber is a terrific material for deep pressure vessels, and he is proud that his company has the data to prove it.

- In July 2025, the Coast Guard will likely release its final report, but unfortunately not in time for me to include it in this book. Honestly, I do not expect much from the report. This is not because of the investigators—who seem like dedicated professionals taking their jobs seriously—but rather because of the lack of contextual evidence and subject matter experts. Then again, I will reserve judgment until I read the report in the coming weeks.

This is not the end of this story. I expect we are just getting started. Stay tuned.

ACKNOWLEDGMENTS

First, I want to thank you, the reader. Your interest in learning more about the OceanGate story is truly inspirational, because it demonstrates a commitment to dig beyond the online glut of clickbait headlines in order to discover a deeper truth. And if you actually paid money for this book (instead of borrowing it from a friend or library), then I owe you an even greater debt of gratitude, because you have helped finance an ongoing legacy of exploration via my royalty donation to charities that support young explorers. I am honestly humbled by your generosity.

Speaking of the *Titan* crew, I hope that this book plays at least a small part in helping to preserve each of their legacies. While I knew Stockton quite well, I spent only a bit of time with Hamish Harding. I flew with him on a Zero-G training flight before his suborbital flight with Blue Origin. I was also there for that launch, which is where I met his wife and son. I know he loved them very much, because he spoke about them a great deal throughout our shared Zero-G flight. I met PH Nargeolet only briefly once, but Stockton raved about him constantly and respected him immensely. And although I never knew Shahzada Dawood or his son, Suleman, I have heard from others who did know them, and they all held both in high regard. All five were true explorers who sadly lost their lives in the pursuit of what they believed was a cause greater than themselves.

Stockton was survived by his wife, Wendy, and his children, grandchildren, sisters, and many friends. They were also a part of my own OceanGate journey—some more directly than others—so I hope this book helps them in some way cope with their tremendous loss.

I could not have made it through those first horrific days in Vienna without the compassionate emotional support of my fellow space entrepreneurs, Barbara Belvisi and Aaron Kemmer, as well as Aaron's fiancée, Angelia Ong, and the BOLD Community leader, Reka Artner. I am also eternally grateful for the brave public efforts of Kyle Bingham, David Concannon, and Richard Garriott during the frantic search and rescue efforts. There were many more people involved whom I did not know, but I am also thankful for their dedicated work. As I fought to navigate the tumultuous global media frenzy of the accident, I was fortunate to get expert advice from Ryan Hayter, Dennis Muilenburg, Miles O'Brien, and George Whitesides, each of whom took time out from their busy lives to share their insights with me.

There are not enough words or pages in this book to describe the sacrifices made by my girlfriend, Carrie, as my personal life raft for the entirety of this tragic experience. This was not the life she would have chosen, but she gave 100 percent of herself to help me through the past year. On more than one occasion, she was the only reason I was able to keep pushing forward.

Although this book focuses primarily on my relationship with Stockton, my OceanGate experience was molded so much by my fellow crew members. Over the years there have been way too many to name here, but if you ever worked with me at OceanGate or the OceanGate Foundation, then hopefully you already know how much you mean to me. Likewise, there were countless explorers, scientists, technologists, and storytellers who joined us for expeditions and dives in *Antipodes*, and every one of you played a part in my journey.

I also want to thank all of the *Titanic* Mission Specialists, most of whom I did not know previously but all of whom welcomed me with open arms after the accident, especially Renata Rojas. I know they are all suffering and still struggling to cope with their loss, so I can only hope that someday I will be able to support them as they have supported me.

On a much broader level, I am grateful to the small, tight-knit global submersible community that took in me and Stockton in the early years, especially those we have lost, such as Pete Hoffmann, Phil Nuytten, Don Walsh, and Chris Welsh. My life would not have been the same without Graham Hawkes, who introduced me to the fascinating world of ocean exploration, submersibles, and, of course, Stockton Rush. I learned how to build subs from Pete Hoffmann, how to pilot a sub from Tym Catterson, how to run surface operations from Ursula Ginster, how to lead expeditions from Rob McCallum, how to navigate complex regulations from Will Kohnen, how to be a maverick from Karl Stanley, and how to inspire confidence from Patrick Lahey. I was admitted into The Explorers Club via the gracious sponsorship of Ken Howery and Don Walsh.

The Ocean Explorers production team, led by my friend Justin Bursch and including Josh Altman, Jeff Leaf, and Grady Sexton, has been incredibly supportive throughout this entire process. Although technically I have been helping them with their film project, it is really they who have helped me find my voice as a storyteller.

The idea for this book came together quite quickly thanks to the expertise of David Meerman Scott, my friend who is a serial best-selling author and with whom I share many common interests, including space, music, rainforest conservation, and, of course, the ocean. He encouraged me to take on this project as part of my grieving process, he gave me early advice on how to write my first book, he introduced me to his (now also my) publisher, and he even came up with the initial title. "Thank you" seems so inadequate in this case.

I also received early advice and encouragement from Kellie Gerardi, Gaelin Rosenwaks, and Kelly Wienersmith, a few of my space/ocean friends who are also successful published authors. I truly appreciated the feedback from Sarah Pousho, who read an early draft of the manuscript, and of course the kind foreword provided by the incomparable Miles O'Brien.

This book would not have seen the light of day were it not for the talented team at BenBella Books, including my publisher, Matt Holt, and my editor, Lydia Choi. They were incredibly patient with me as a first-time author, especially given the extremely sensitive subject matter.

When I was six years old, my parents left behind their lives in Argentina to give me and my siblings a better life in the United States, and without their unfathomable sacrifice and lifelong support, I never would have had this amazing life journey.

Likewise, my ex-wife, Julie, gamely agreed to a couple of highly disruptive cross-country family relocations during our OceanGate experience, and she even worked at OceanGate for a brief time. None of it was easy for her, but she played a key role in making all of this possible.

Finally, my three incredible kids—Rebecca, Daniel, and Caleb—have always been an inspiration that makes me want to be a role model worthy of their love and respect. They knew Stockton and dived in *Antipodes*, so this story has been extremely personal for them. I hope I can help them achieve their own life goals while also leaving this world a better place for them.

ABOUT THE AUTHOR

GUILLERMO SÖHNLEIN is an explorer, entrepreneur, investor, and philanthropist with a particular passion for space, oceans, and sustainability. Over the course of a twenty-five-year entrepreneurial career, he has helped launch over a dozen for-profit ventures and nonprofit organizations. His startups include Space Angels Network in 2006, OceanGate in 2009, and the Humans2Venus Foundation in 2020. He enjoys sharing his experiences with others as an advisor, mentor, board member, teacher, and speaker.

Guillermo earned his AB in economics from the University of California at Berkeley and his JD from the University of California San Francisco College of the Law. He served as an officer in the US Marine Corps and was admitted to The Explorers Club in 2012. Born in Buenos Aires, Argentina, he was raised in Silicon Valley and currently splits his time between Barcelona in Spain and Atlanta in the United States. He is the proud father of three grown children.